Conflict And Cooperation:
Reflections On The New Deal In Texas

Edited by
Milton S. Jordan and George M. Cooper

STEPHEN F. AUSTIN STATE UNIVERSITY PRESS
2019

Copyright © 2019 by Stephen F. Austin State University

All rights reserved. For information about permission to reproduce selections from this book write to Permissions:

Cover image: *The Last Crop,* a mural in the Linden Post Office painted by New Deal artist Victor Arnautoff

STEPHEN F. AUSTIN STATE UNIVERSITY PRESS
PO Box 13007, SFA Station
Nacogdoches, TX 75962
sfapress@sfasu.edu
936-468-1078

For information about special discounts for bulk purchases, please contact Texas A&M University Press Consortium
tamupress.com

ISBN: 978-1-62288-228-1

First Edition

Contents

Foreword / 5
    Kyle Wilkison

Introduction / 9
    Milton Jordan and George Cooper

PART I THE NEW DEAL IN TEXAS

"Too Hard for Women:" New Deal Work Relief Programs and Texas Women / 13
    Cynthia Brandimarte

New Deal Programs Supporting the Visual Arts in Texas / 28
    Victoria H. and Light Townsend Cummins

South Texans in Washington during the New Deal / 38
    George Cooper

Eleanor Roosevelt and a Woman's New Deal in Texas / 48
    Mary Scheer

"The Yield on This Investment Should be High": The National Youth Administration in Texas / 65
    Carroll Scogin-Brincefield

PART II THE NEW DEAL AND TEXAS COMMUNITIES

I Too Sing "Texas, Our Texas": Texas African Americans and the New Deal / 81
    Ronald E. Goodwin

The Construction of Huntsville State Park: Race and Recovery in Twentieth Century East Texas / 89
    Carolyn A. Carroll and Jeff Littlejohn

"Nature Has Provided a Park in the Rough": Caddo Lake and the CCC / 108
    Milton Jordan

The New Deal in Cass County, Texas, 1933-1943 / 117
Brenda Taylor Matthews

"We Patch Anything":
WPA Sewing Rooms in Fort Worth / 131
Susan Allen Kline

Texas Historical Memory: The Curious Case
of the Princeton FSA Migratory Labor Camp / 143
Keith Volanto

Notes on Contributors / 152

Foreword

Kyle Wilkison

For most of the twentieth century, George Washington Smith cut hair for a living in the small East Texas hamlet of Grand Saline. When I met him in the early 1980s, the energetic nonagenarian Socialist could still get worked up over the Wilson Administration's prosecution of Kate Richard O'Hare. On the other hand, he saw Franklin D. Roosevelt as America's Moses whose New Deal led the nation out of the economic wilderness. Smith believed the New Deal saved the country and he had local examples to prove it. From Social Security to the new paint on farmers' houses, it was all the New Deal. "Roosevelt stole our program," he said wryly. Roosevelt himself would object to that claim, as do economists and historians, but Smith's enthusiastic endorsement reveals the power of the New Deal within the memories of many Texans who lived it.

The New Deal grew, in part, from the realization among the political class of the obvious risks in allowing the working class alone to bear the weight of a broken economy. Who could say what potential revolutionary dangers lurked ahead? Among the nostrums on offer in the early 1930s, the New Deal threatened the least disruption to the existing structure of wealth distribution. For the business class and their representatives, relying on government to restart the market may have been bitter medicine in the abstract, but, if it saved capitalism, it would be worth it.

Whatever the class interests and short-term pragmatic goals of its architects, those on the receiving end of the New Deal viewed it through their own lenses. They formulated meanings that jibed with their own experiences or bespoke their deepest yearnings. Since almost everyone in 1930s Texas tasted, or observed, the dreary widespread pain of the Depression, it is remarkable that the New Deal has not attracted more historians of Texas. Perhaps it is because an accurate accounting of the New Deal would focus attention on people without a history.

One of my undergraduate mentors gravely explained that the poor majority did not have a history. According to my teacher, they did nothing to make history, nothing much happened to them and, most important, nothing changed. Such a view complements the last century of Texas historiography.

The working-class majority yet awaits its historian; but, while we wait, this volume adds dramatically to the short shelf of books paying attention to ordinary Texans. Herein, mixed with politicians and a few luminaries, the reader discovers working people, unemployed people, working class women, African Americans and Tejanos, seamstresses, farmers, teachers, artists, and others from among the common lot. Telling the experiences of such people and their interaction with the New Deal challenges at least three strong Texas myths.

What if the poor majority appreciated and derived benefit from government programs? An accounting of the alacrity with which desperate Texans latched on to any number of New Deal efforts contradicts our popular self-image as tough-as-a-bootstrap individualists like nothing has since the Runaway Scrape. The second challenge embedded in New Deal history lies in the tacit admission that free-market capitalism had not performed as advertised. The New Deal's proposed structural fixes came from capitalism's best thinkers seeking a pragmatic and politically feasible means to save the economy from continuing its downward trajectory as well as heading off potential social disorder. The third way in which studying New Deal history challenges the conventional narrative is that it conclusively explodes the staggeringly wrong-headed notion that Texas history ends in 1900 and nothing of importance happened in the twentieth century.

In a 2010 journal article, Keith Volanto, whose essay concludes this volume, challenged the field with his "Where are the New Deal Historians of Texas?" Volanto covers the existing work but concentrates on identifying the wide, gaping holes in the historiography of New Deal Texas. He speculates that "[w]riting about government action to solve an economic crisis in Texas . . . simply does not have much appeal" within Texas' supposedly anti-government mainstream culture.[1] But, help was on the way.

Beginning in 2013, co-editor George Cooper began organizing annual New Deal history symposia across the state in an ongoing effort that continues. After six years, this volume features the fruit of these annual efforts. Alongside the annual New Deal conferences, there is another element to the origin of this work. In a 2011 essay, co-editor Milton Jordan called for a fresh look at the Texas past even as he suggested an explanation for its current state. Battle sites are "usually well preserved. The stories of how we fought with one another are oft retold." However, Jordan calls on historians to chronicle "those places where sharing and cooperation were the tactics, and where the people's strategy was to create or recreate community. Look for those places. Tell those stories."[2]

The people herein, their places and their stories, point us toward a more accurate rendering of the past. As a bonus, their stories reveal a past more interesting, complicated, rich and human than any myth.

[1] Keith Volanto, "Where are the New Deal Historians of Texas? A Literature Review of the New Deal Experience in Texas," *East Texas Historical Journal:* Vol. 48, No. 2, Article 7. Available at: https://scholarworks.sfasu.edu/ethj/vol48/iss. 2/7.

[2] Milton Jordan, (2011) "A River Creeps Through It," *East Texas Historical Journal:* Vol. 49, No. 1, Article 7. Available at: https://scholarworks.sfasu.edu/ethj/vol49/iss. 1/7.

Introduction

Milton S. Jordan and George M. Cooper

From its beginnings in the spring of 1933 to its close with U.S. entry into World War II the New Deal had a significant impact on the state of Texas. The projects and programs of this federal recovery effort influenced the culture, economy, social structures and politics of the state. In Texas, as in other states, many New Deal programs created their share of disagreement. Some of these were conflicts over local versus federal control. Others were along long-standing local divides. Some were verbally and a few physically violent. The deep and widespread need of the time, however, and the obvious help available from federal dollars overcame most disagreements.

In this collection of eleven essays the editors seek to highlight some examples of the lasting positive impact of these New Deal projects and programs. We have organized these essays into two sections. Part one includes more general studies considering literature on women's roles in the Texas New Deal, programs across the state and some of the personalities involved. Part two looks at specific local projects supported by several of the numerous New Deal agencies. In their essays the writers challenge the currently popular view that "government is the problem." In case after case they demonstrate the positive role these federal programs filled in the lives of individuals and the communities in which they lived and worked.

The editors want to acknowledge the contribution of the Texas New Deal Symposium, sponsored by the East Texas Historical Association, for its role in reinvigorating New Deal scholarship within the State of Texas. Many of the participants in that periodic celebration of the New Deal are also contributors to this volume. We are also very grateful to all the writers for their contributions, their research in producing them and their efforts in tracking down images that illustrate Texas New Deal Programs. We also thank Kyle Wilkison for writing the Foreword, Cynthia Beeman for help with formatting and Anne Jordan for proofreading and technical assistance. Jennifer Carpenter at Texas Parks and Wildlife has been helpful in numerous ways.

Director Kimberly Verhines of Stephen F. Austin State University Press and Senior Editor, Sarah D. Johnson, took our less than perfect efforts and turned them into a book. We thank them.

Part One:
The New Deal in Texas

"Too Hard for Women":
New Deal Work Relief Programs and Texas Women

Cynthia Brandimarte

On a day in 1939, a junior case worker, Mrs. Carmen Lawrence, sat in a courthouse office in Ballinger, a town in Runnels County, Texas, reviewing applications for work relief. The applicants came from the towns of Winters, Miles, Norton, and Ballinger, and all needed help. Once good for crops and cattle grazing, the land now sustained primarily sheep and goats often sold at rock-bottom prices. Even the discovery of oil in the county some ten years earlier offered no reason for optimism among county residents in the depths of the Great Depression.

Having to cope with ever-changing federal rules, Lawrence buckled down that day to determine which applicants qualified for receiving cash, commodities, temporary work, or failed to qualify for any assistance. She had listened to their stories and recorded what she could on government forms: whether the applicant was a town or rural resident, the number in the household, if the applicant was "Negro" or Mexican, and if he or she was a citizen. During an interview of each applicant, Lawrence had to ask if there was someone in the household who was physically able to work, received a pension, or had insurance. After home visits, she described how homes looked, how clothes appeared, and the condition of furnishings, especially mattresses and bedding. Always looking for evidence of self-sufficiency, workers like Lawrence noted if a household also had a garden.

Lawrence paid special attention to women applicants, though she'd heard it all: women abandoned by husbands; fathers who locked up a family's food so that his wife and kids could not eat; a wandering wife whose husband had left and needed work relief, even though her children were determined to be too young to have a mother working out of the home.[1] A non-resident woman who described herself as feeble-minded, whose husband had been committed to an insane asylum in East Texas, and whose infant was "an idiot" asked Lawrence to locate her mother, a Runnels County resident, whom she had not seen in some twenty years but whose help she now needed desperately. Lawrence was acquainted with the mother, a Ballinger relief applicant, and knew that the woman could help neither her daughter nor her granddaughter. And then there was the Holland case. Bootlegging had barely supported a man named Holland and his wife, but even that income was lost when he died in a car accident. WPA was the widow's only hope, because waitressing jobs were non-existent for women her age.

Carmen Lawrence could not help but muse about the lucky ones—desperate "employables" she could certify as eligible for work relief.[2] Pursuant to WPA procedures, she notified these persons of the kind of work assignment, job duration, and wage they would receive, even though it might be reduced. Fortunate to have her secure position, Lawrence wondered if the women she "certified" would get work in time to feed their families and hold on to jobs long enough to do them some good, not to mention receive adequate pay. She presided over just one county and guessed it was much the same in the other 253 Texas counties mired in economic Depression. At the end of her day, Lawrence wondered if it was simply too hard for women to obtain work relief sufficient for their needs.[3]

INTRODUCTION

When the federal government stepped in to assist large numbers of impoverished and unemployed Americans during the Great Depression, it found itself in uncharted territory. Starting with the dual goals of lifting the spirits and the livelihoods of Americans suffering economic privation, the federal government's effort was light on details. Nonetheless, agencies came to life, morphed, changed names, and sometimes merged.[4] Agency after agency added people to its rolls as others left them. The trial-and-error nature of President Roosevelt's work relief experiment, plus limited communications during the 1930s, made it difficult for Americans to learn about and understand federal programs in time to benefit from them. Nevertheless, and despite rapid changes in programs and policies, some, though certainly not all, of the needy got opportunities to work.

The federal program with which I am most familiar, the Civilian Conservation Corps (CCC), was the first program, though it was originally designed only for men.[5] The CCC employed men to tackle soil erosion, address conservation issues, and construct parks. I cannot help but wish that Eleanor Roosevelt's She-She-She camps had become a robust partner to the CCC nor resist imagining what a female CCC counterpart might have looked like. A few attempts to create CCC-like work camps for women in Texas and elsewhere did not concentrate on work projects, but instead on teaching women practical skills.[6] Although limited in funding, scope, and longevity, this and other New Deal women's work relief programs did eventually provide relief for some women.

A FEW NUMBERS

The number of people in Texas who benefitted from New Deal programs, including direct relief or work relief, is estimated to be in the tens of thousands. Women are among the total, but their stories are easy to overlook because of the scattered nature of historical sources, varied programs, inevitable slippages between federal, state, and local implementation, and the fact that far fewer women than men received direct aid or employment. Comparatively few in number, women beneficiaries are hard to locate. However, these are hardly reasons not to try.[7] My hope is that this overview encourages researchers to identify women beneficiaries and give them voice.

How did American women fare in New Deal work relief programs? As indicated, far fewer women than men gained employment in federal programs. Disparities between employed female and male workers widened or narrowed depending upon programs, federal dollars allocated to fund them, and the extent of matching state and local funds. Still, there was never a time when disparities were other than gaping. To illustrate, in 1934 the Federal Emergency Relief Administration (FERA) began to create educational and work camps for unemployed women, but they aided no more than 3,000 girls at a time when almost 1.5 million girls and women were seeking relief.[8] During its tenure, by comparison, the CCC absorbed between 2.5 and 3 million boys and men but had places for only 8,500 women. The Works Progress Administration (later the Work Projects Administration, or WPA) employed over 8 million Americans but only 12% of its budget was directed to women, hiring 372,000 of the nation's 3 million unemployed women.[9] In the National Youth Administration's (NYA) out-of-school work program in Texas, young women briefly held a majority of the NYA's work relief positions; most of the time they held an estimated 45% of the positions.[10] Women fared somewhat better in Federal Project One that employed writers, musicians, artists, and actors in creative fields.[11]

GENDER, CLASS, AND RACE

The New Deal was a mixed bag for women. For some, it provided a chance to work in federal service and the public arena. Elite women were appointed to leadership positions in New Deal agencies. Their educations, participations in the Democratic Party, advocacies of suffrage, and experiences in social welfare fields had put them in contact with each other and brought them to the attention of the Roosevelt administration, including, of course, that of First Lady Eleanor. Molly Dewson led the Woman's Division of the Democratic National Committee; Frances Perkins served as FDR's Secretary of Labor; Ellen S. Woodward became the first director of the newly created Women's Division and later director of the Service and Professional Program of the WPA; and, an active member of the NYA's National Advisory Committee, Mary McLeod Bethune directed its Division of Negro Affairs.[12]

Women who were neither educated nor well connected had few if any such opportunities. For them, New Deal programs often overlooked their needs to work to support themselves and, in many cases, their families. Regarded as mothers first and as workers a distant second, women were considered only for jobs deemed suitable for women and for which they were usually paid less than jobs assigned to men paid. While men were hired to build roads and parks, women were enlisted to wash laundry and can food.

More often than men, women found their job assignments shortened in duration or their wages cut. At one point, the federal government required that if a married couple were both federal employees, the wife had to resign her post.[13] Because men's jobs often earned more than women's did, and because employed women were seen as extraneous by some, policies and gender bias caused women to lose jobs.

Not only were women's positions gendered and often tenuous, class resentments were part of the picture. Letters penned to Eleanor Roosevelt occasionally expressed gratitude that women like Perkins and Woodward were in influential national positions or at least close to them. Locally, however, it was usually a different story. Some workers resented women in leadership positions. For example, unemployed professional women with supervisory experience were put in charge of sewing rooms, much to the chagrin of seamstresses who may have known that the supervisor was not in desperate straits or had an employed spouse. Alternately, trained librarians, unemployed and certified to work for the WPA Library Project supervised untrained WPA "certifieds" and found them too unskilled to follow exacting instructions.

Anglo women faced fewer biases than black and Mexican women when applying for work relief. After southern Democrats insisted on local administration of many federal programs, Jim Crow segregationists across the South had power to control hiring practices. Segregated occupations for African American women persisted in federal programs despite a policy that forbade discrimination. Perhaps assuming ongoing economic hardships, the largely male New Deal program administrators regarded only African American women as permanent workers, and the Household Workers Training Project was designed to train them for employment as domestic helpers.

1.1 Food service was also considered "appropriate" for women's work relief, especially for the unskilled. Here, four women gained employment with the School Lunch Program in Crosbyton, Crosby County. The WPA workers served some 224 noon meals each day; most students ate free. Flickr http://bit.ly/TexasWPAPhotos.

Perversely, the Housekeeping Aide Project was open to all women, regardless of race, though workers in it performed the same duties as those in the former Project.[14] Mexican American women were given a few more occupational choices than African American women were given. While WPA adult educational courses tended to focus on citizenship, Mexican American women could also receive clerical training. In any event, most of them in San Antonio sought jobs in sewing rooms rather than enrolling in WPA classes.[15]

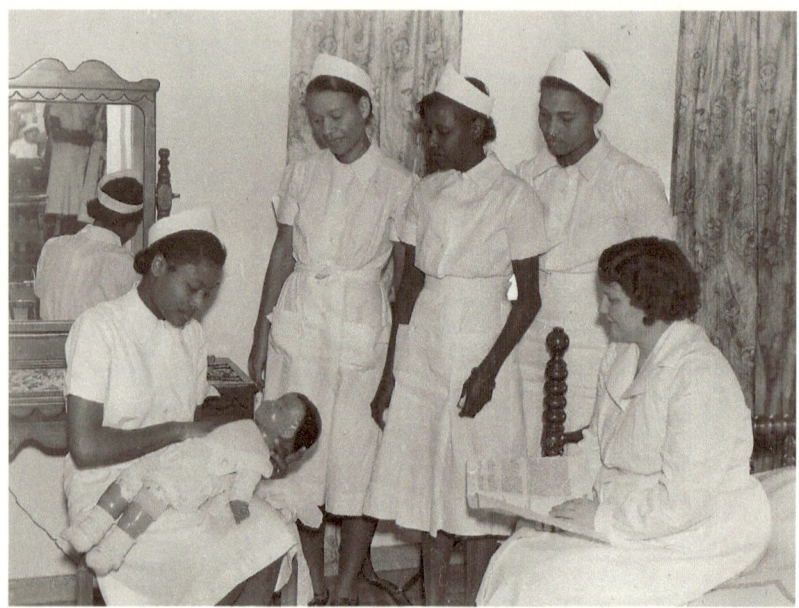

1.2   This image captures the teacher and students during a childcare class in the Household Workers Training Project in Dallas, c. 1940. The four black students appear to be tutored in what many considered their inevitable occupation as domestic workers. In contrast, women in the Housekeeping Aide Project were temporarily assigned to assist impoverished families when there was a death, illness, or acute need; they cooked, washed, cleaned, and cared for newborns and the infirm, fulfilling many of the tasks the trainees were learning. Flickr http://bit.ly/TexasWPAPhotos.

Overall, some regarded the goals of women's programs as fuzzy and having few visible lasting results. Because male policymakers viewed women as temporary workers, training tended to focus on acquiring skills that would come in handy for the eventual running of a household and not on acquiring skills for future employment outside the home. Ever on the lookout for saving money, critics of the New Deal questioned funding programs to train women to run a household. Absent training for future employment in occupations—even for women—New Deal programs were vulnerable to budget cuts. To better position themselves budgetarily, programs, especially those that employed women, shifted their emphasis and began to highlight the value of the services they trained women to perform in communities.[16]

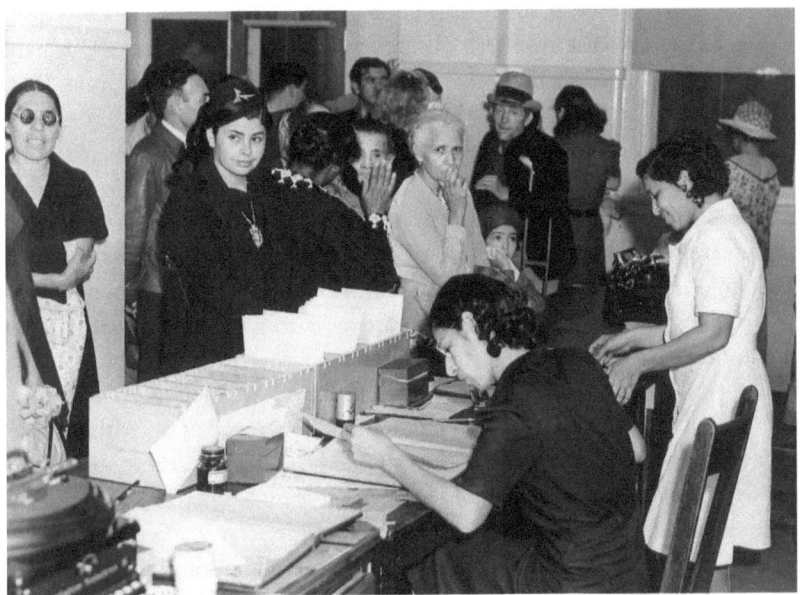

1.3   Some Mexican American women did work in clerical jobs. Margarita Motes, a WPA Junior Clerk, and Mary Louise Jiménez, a WPA Clerk, registered approximately 200 clients daily at the Out-Patient Clinic in the Robert B. Green Hospital in San Antonio, 1940. Flickr http://bit.ly/TexasWPAPhotos

SCHOLARS LOOK AT TEXAS

It would be folly to think that in the relatively sparse field of Texas New Deal history, there would be a clutch of studies covering Texas women during the New Deal or a clutch covering the still smaller category of Texas women who were hired in work relief programs.[17] To date, few historians have scrutinized either.

Julia K. Blackwelder's *Women of the Depression: Caste and Culture in San Antonio, 1929-1939*, published in 1984, remains the only book-length study of women in Texas during the Great Depression.[18] The author deftly presents and interprets data about San Antonio's women workers during the Great Depression. Blackwelder argues that issues of caste and culture determined the ways individual groups of women experienced the Great Depression, both as workers and family members. She observes that African American, Mexican American, and Anglo women had different opportunities at different stages of their lives. She contends that "generalizations about the national Depression experience camouflage the realities of the 1930s for individual groups."[19] For anyone pursuing the study of Texas women during the Great Depression, this is required reading, and Chapters 5, 7, and 10 are especially relevant to this overview. Blackwelder's observations about women in 1930s San Antonio can be applied to those living elsewhere, and she urges that ethnicity and class be factored in whenever we are tempted to generalize about women during the Depression.

A history of the National Youth Administration by Carol A. Weisenberger provides a mostly positive view of the NYA in Texas because of the nondiscrimination policy of its Executive Director, Aubrey W. Williams, and the participation of Lyndon B. Johnson. Weisenberger sets out to discover whether the NYA served as "a tool of social reform" and concludes that it did indeed do so.[20] In a chapter titled "'Blazing New Trails'—New Opportunities for Minorities and Women in Texas," she argues that the NYA was more enlightened than some of the other New Deal programs, despite often being stymied by local discriminatory attitudes. Most helpful in providing statistics about NYA women workers, along with African American and Mexican American workers, the chapter ends with a brief summary of the accomplishments and the shortfalls of the NYA in Texas.

Long a student of the WPA and a professional librarian, Jane Warner Rogers published two articles in *Texas Libraries* about federal work relief programs that hired women. Both the WPA Statewide Library Project and its Historical Records Survey Project, which was initially part of the WPA Writers Program, capture Rogers' interest.[21] In particular, she discusses the expenditures and scale of the former Project. During its five years of operation, more than $6 million in federal funds was spent on the Library Project, mending books well worn by patrons, opening school libraries, and expanding public services to communities previously unserved. At its most active, the program employed more than 2,000 workers in over 1,500 locations in Texas.[22] Although Rogers' focus is not specifically on women, she is well aware that women made up a large percentage of this occupational group: "it [library work] was suitable not only for librarians but also for former clerical and secretarial workers, retail clerks, and housewives who had never sought work before."[23] Overall, this is a well-researched summary of the Library Project's accomplishments.

In her article, "Records Survey Attempt to Inventory County Records," Rogers continues her inquiry into the multi-faceted efforts of the WPA.[24] She offers a short account of how the Historical Records Survey came about, how it was administered and organized, the Texas counties whose records were inventoried, and the disposition of those records. She concludes that spread too thinly, survey workers were unable to finish one project before having to begin others. The names of project's leaders show up in her article, but more in-depth research is needed to identify those of WPA employees.

The present volume includes two articles about Texas women during the Great Depression.[25] Mary L. Scheer focuses on Eleanor Roosevelt and women in the Texas New Deal; her contribution on the First Lady serves as a counterpoint to Susan Kline's study of WPA sewing rooms, the most ubiquitous work relief project for unskilled women in the state. These two studies—one, of a singular distinguished figure and another, of numerous unnamed seamstresses from Marshall to El Paso—are engaging bookends for shelves still needing to be filled.

STUDENTS LOOK AT TEXAS: THESES AND DISSERTATIONS

Texas had its share of colleges and universities whose faculty members were deeply involved with New Deal program activities. This was especially true at locations where there was an institution of higher learning and a nearby WPA district office. Faculty at colleges and universities in Texas guided MA theses and PhD dissertations in History, Sociology, Education, Library Science, and other disciplines. Those studying during the Great Depression carried out fairly narrow studies of the period.[26] Graduate students looked at the New Deal landscape while the federal programs were in progress, rather than their completed results. Nevertheless, their research may contain archival data for current researchers to investigate.

A number of bibliographies of theses and dissertations on the New Deal not only list pre-World War II studies, but also sketch the trajectory of those works and the renewed interest in the New Deal that took hold during the late 1960s and the 1970s. Janaki Srinivasan has taken stock of PhD Dissertations and Master's Theses pertaining to the New Deal written in US universities (January 2012): *https://livingnewdeal.org/wp-content/uploads/2012/01/NewDeal-Thesis-Bibliography-v3.pdf*. Another stocktaking, which focuses on Texas, has been provided by Steve Issner (2001): *https://livingnewdeal.org/wp-content/uploads/2012/03/Texas-1-3.pdf*.

As part of a "second wave" of interest in New Deal topics, returning graduate student Jane Warner Rogers wrote "WPA Professional and Service Projects In Texas" as her thesis in History at the University of Texas at Austin in 1976.[27] I find her work to be most helpful in providing an overview of the programs within the WPA that hired a large number of women in Texas during the Great Depression. Having published the two previously noted short articles on aspects of the Professional and

Service Projects of the WPA, Rogers undertook her thesis on the WPA Division that administered "white collar" work. She begins by saying that construction projects were highly visible and often cornerstones marking the role of the WPA, other federal programs, and local sponsoring agencies or groups. Non-construction projects were less visible and known. Rogers examines efforts ranging from the Adult Education, Toy, and Housekeeping Aide projects to Flood Control, Statewide Tax Survey, and Mineral Resources projects. She briefly describes them one by one and calls for local history studies to amplify her overview. She also encourages disciplinary histories of specific projects. These have been most successful with Project One—art, theatre, and music. In large part, however, Rogers's call for further research remains unanswered.

FUTURE RESEARCH

There are a number of ways to pursue the topic of Texas women aided by federal work relief programs during the Great Depression. Examining an occupational group, a program, a location, or a discipline would be one way to begin. Identifying workers in them would be of lasting value. Every publication and student report mentioned here includes the names of leaders and sometimes those of workers. The names of workers also surface in the Historical Records Survey at UT-Austin's Briscoe Center: Mrs. Ida A. Schweppe, Mrs. Carl James, Mrs. Nellie Morris, Annie Gerber, Melinda Rankin, Catherine Deaver, and Carolyn M. McBride.[28] Annie Taylor, Jewel Randle, Wilma Petersen, Ruby Maloney, Sara Lacy, and Florence Mathis appear as workers in the Writers Program of the WPA.[29] But why not crowd-source the names of Texas women in New Deal work relief programs and see what patterns emerge after biographical research?

A cautionary note is in order, however. Not all occupational groups are as well documented and organized as the Library Project. Not all collections are as complete as the Runnels County records or contain the descriptive documentation supplied by Carmen Lawrence. By no means are all workers likely to leave a paper trail as did Mary K. Taylor, who was director of women's work in Texas. Nor, needless to say, did they undergo oral history interviews like that given by Florence Fenley of Uvalde, who worked for the WPA Writers Project.[30]

1.4   Library Project. A large and varied project in Texas, the Library Progra m is well documented photographically as well as textually. In this image WPA worker Odessa Fisher checks out a book to WPA teacher Essie A. Davis at Texarkana's "Colored" Public Library, 1940. For a photographic survey of the WPA in Texas visit Flickr http://bit.ly/TexasWPAPhotos.

CONCLUSION

It is difficult enough to identify Texas women who were employed by President Roosevelt's New Deal programs and understand their experiences. It is even more challenging to identify those who benefited from the programs less directly. As Carmen Lawrence knew, there were wives, sisters, and daughters who received commodities—food, clothing, and household goods; and there were women who could pay the rent because their sons, brothers, and husbands earned a wage by building roads in a county. And those women who found private sector jobs—as waitresses, domestics, clerks—may have helped the federal government extend a hand to those who could not find such jobs.

But because Texas women during the New Deal may be hard to find is no reason to think they are irretrievably lost. Because the positions Texas women held were conventional and gendered does not mean that that is all they were. In fact, scholars and policymakers are looking anew at the topic of women and the New Deal. The Living New Deal, an association headquartered in California, sponsored a conference shortly before this volume went to press. The program offered a comparative approach to the 1930s New Deal and a more recent "New Deal." Scholar Eileen Boris presented "Toward a New New Deal… and the Women Shall Lead" session. Discussants opined that the New New Deal will be led by women, especially working-class women who currently form a considerable part of the labor force, including organized unions. Not the prosperous and well-connected suffragettes, but grassroots activists engaged in the social welfare movement are mobilizing.[31]

The phrase "too hard for women" was used by one state's Civil Works Administrator, who expressed his belief that outdoor beautification work was too strenuous for women's work relief because it required raking. Others were offended by the implication that women were physically delicate or weak. After all, any woman who had farmed and had routinely plowed fields and chopped wood could most assuredly wield a rake.[32] Some work tasks were demanding physically, especially once defense industries ramped up and women worked in metal and machine shops.[33] None of those tasks were beyond the physical capabilities of the women who welcomed the opportunity to perform them. We know today that such work was not too difficult for women to accomplish, but during the Great Depression work relief was just too hard to get and too hard to keep for many Texas women.

Notes and Acknowledgments

[1] Some married couples divorced during the Great Depression in order for the two spouses to apply separately for relief and thus double the chance of receiving federal relief. This practice gave rise to the phrase "Depression divorces." However, when the family's situation was widely known in the community, the stories were likely legitimate.

[2] Martha H. Swain, Ellen S. Woodward: *New Deal Advocate for Women* (Jackson: University Press of Mississippi, 1995), 54. Here Swain explains that direct relief was intended for "unemployables" or those "certified as too old, disabled, or incompetent to work." Those who were certified as "employables" were eligible "to work on projects of public and social value."

[3] The author has woven together several clients' stories as recorded by case worker Mrs. Carmen Lawrence. The documentation is contained in the Runnels County (Texas) New Deal Agencies Collection, 1933-1943, Dolph Briscoe Center for American History, The University of Texas at Austin. This individual's name is recorded as Carmer Laurence in the United States Population Census, Runnels County, Texas, 1940, Sheet 20B. Living in a household consisting of her husband and two grown daughters, she identified herself as a WPA field worker.

[4] In Woodward, Swain observes: "Further confusion awaits anyone who tries to keep straight the administration of federal relief programs, after termination of the CWA [Civil Works Administration], all projects reverted to the states under the 'Emergency Work Relief Program'", 51.

[5] Cynthia Brandimarte (with Angela Reed), *Texas State Parks and the CCC: The Legacy of the Civilian Conservation Corps* (College Station: Texas A&M University, 2013).

[6] Susan Ware, *Beyond Suffrage: Women in the New Deal* (Cambridge: Harvard University, 1981), 112-13.

[7] Such an investigation about the numbers of women who were employed in New Deal agencies in Texas would surely benefit from the papers of WPA State Director H.P. Drought. But as long as the collection eludes researchers, they must be dogged and resourceful.

[8] Carol A. Weisenberger, *Dollars and Dreams: The National Youth Administration in Texas* (Peter Lang International, 1994), 142-43.

[9] http://fdr4freedoms.org/wp-content/themes/fdf4fdr/DownloadablePDFs/II_HopeRecoveryReform/15_WomenandtheNewDeal.pdf, 7.

[10] Evan McCarty Arendell, "Crossing into Bounty: Blacks, Women, Mexicans and the Texas NYA" (master's thesis, Tarleton State University, 1994), 48.

[11] However, some feared that this creative WPA may have resulted in cuts to the institutional and community-service projects of the WPA that provided work relief for unskilled and professional women in white collar jobs; see Swain in Woodward, 104-5. Swain further notes in Woodward, "Any assessment of the WPA women's programs should go beyond tallying percentages of women on work relief or indicting WPA policies as discriminatory against women", 105.

[12] Ware, *Beyond Suffrage*. Ware deftly explains how networks of women had formed through the experiences of gaining the vote in 1920 and later how this coterie advanced the needs of impoverished women and unemployed women in the 1930s and beyond. On work relief for women, see especially 105-115 in Ware.

[13] http://fdr4freedoms.org/wp-content/themes/fdf4fdr/DownloadablePDFs/II_HopeRecoveryReform/15_WomenandtheNewDeal.pdf, 7.

[14] Julia Kirk Blackwelder, *Women of the Depression: Caste and Culture in San Anonio, 1929-1939* (College Station: Texas A&M University, 1984), 110. Black household aid workers did assist in African American households.

[15] Blackwelder, 124. For information relevant to Mexican American women and the NYA, see Arendell, 67, who cites Dallek, 138, to make the point that LBJ and his NYA failed to promote Mexican youths to the extent that they had blacks and women.

[16] Georgina Hickey, "'The Lowest Form of Work Relief'': Authority, Gender, and the State in Atlanta's WPA Sewing Rooms", 18, in Elna C. Green, *The New Deal and Beyond: Social Welfare in the South since 1930* (Athens: University of Georgia, 2003). Hickey cites one account that sees the shift in the name change from Works Progress Administration to Work Projects Administration. In Texas, this shift is visible in the May 20-25, 1940, publicity campaign "This Work Pays Your Community" discussed in Jane Warner Rogers, "WPA Professional and Service Projects In Texas" (master's thesis, The University of Texas at Austin, 1976).

[17] Keith Volanto, "Where are the New Deal Historians of Texas?: A Literature Review of the New Deal Experience in Texas," *East Texas Historical Journal* 48 (Fall 2010): 41-57.

[18] Blackwelder, *Women of the Depression*.

[19] Blackwelder, 168.

[20] Weisenberger, 6.

[21] Jane Warner Rogers, "The WPA Statewide Library Project in Texas," *Texas Libraries* 34 (Winter 1972): 209-218; and "Records Survey Attempt to Inventory County Records," *Texas Libraries* 37 (Fall 1975): 129-143. For an account of earlier state efforts to preserve local records, see Martha Doty Freeman, "Preservation of Texas's Public Records, a Vital Work in Progress," *Information*

& Culture 49 (no. 1, 2014): 90-107.

²² Rogers, "Library," 209. See Notes 4 and 5.

²³ Rogers, "Library," 210.

²⁴ Rogers, "Survey."

²⁵ Another contributor to the present volume, Light Townsend Cummins, has authored *Allie Victoria Tennant and the Visual Arts in Dallas* (College Station: Texas A&M University, 2015). Artist Tennant worked on a number of public art projects including several for the WPA.

²⁶ For an example of such a focused study, see Lucile Jaeggli Martin, "A Study of the Homemaking Education and Training Program for Out-of-School Youth Employed by the National Youth Administration in Texas" (master's thesis, University of Texas at Austin, 1943).

²⁷ Jane Warner Rogers, "WPA Professional and Service Projects In Texas", 1976. Another example of studies of this era is Deborah Lynn Self, "The National Youth Administration in Texas, 1935-1939" (master's thesis, Texas Tech University, 1974). Neither Rogers nor Self focus exclusively on women.

²⁸ Works Progress Administration records, Historical Records Survey, Dolph Briscoe Center for American History, The University of Texas at Austin, Box 4G224.

²⁹ Texas Writers Project records, Texas State Library and Archives Commission, Boxes 1962/218-11 and -6.

³⁰ Fenley, Florence Oral History Interview, August 11, 1970. Interview by Paul Patterson. Southwest Collection/Special Collections Library.

³¹ Jennifer L. Carpenter, colleague and conference attendee, shared these observations with the author. Please see https://livingnewdeal.org/women-and-the-spirit-of-the-new-deal-conference. A brochure of the same title as the conference contains a list of women throughout the US who are known to have been active in the New Deal and many were leaders in a variety of efforts during the 1930s.

³² Swain, Woodward, 46-47.

³³ Weisenberger, 146.

The author is grateful to the following individuals for their assistance: Jennifer Carpenter, Martha Freeman, Margaret Schlankey, Kathryn Kenefick, Tonia Wood, and Richard Gilreath.

Record Group 69's Texan WPA photos may now be viewed on Flickr, under the username @txparksccc or the title, "Texas and the WPA." Visit http://bit.ly/TexasWPAPhotos to browse thousands of images of our state's New Deal projects, structures, and workers.

New Deal Programs Supporting the Visual Arts in Texas

Victoria H. Cummins and Light Townsend Cummins

Federal funding invigorated the visual arts across Texas and the rest of the nation during the Great Depression. These New Deal art programs focused on giving individual artists hourly wages or commissions to produce paintings, murals, sculptures, bas-reliefs, and other forms of art. This art embellished post offices, schools, university campuses, federal buildings, courthouses, city halls, airports, and similar public places. Most New Deal-sponsored art in Texas manifested a distinctive, colorful, and representational style which even today makes it recognizable to everyone who sees it.[1] Texas received more than its fair share of Federal support for the visual arts during the New Deal. That was because, in addition to national New Deal art programs, the Lone Star state received an increased amount of Federal funding for artistic production because 1936 also marked the centennial of the Texas Revolution against Mexico. Thanks in part to the influence of Texans serving in the Congress and in the administration of Franklin D. Roosevelt, including Vice President John Nance Garner, Senator Tom Connally, Congressman Sam Rayburn, and Houstonian Jesse Jones, the Federal government provided millions of dollars for underwriting this celebration. New Deal support for Texas centennial projects included the construction of buildings, memorials, monuments, museums, and decorating various other public facilities with works of art.[2]

The original idea for the New Deal programs supporting the visual arts came from George Biddle, a well-established Philadelphia artist who had been a classmate of President Roosevelt at Groton and Harvard. During trips to Mexico, Biddle became impressed with the financial support which the Mexican government gave artists to underwrite the creation of murals and other forms of public art. Biddle accordingly wrote his friend Franklin Roosevelt several months after the start of the new administration, suggesting the Federal government provide financial support for public art as part of the New Deal. The president agreed and assembled a group of New Deal advisors to implement such a program.[3] President Roosevelt proved very excited about the prospects for Federal support of the arts as part of the New Deal. "One hundred years from now," he proudly noted, "my administration will be known for its art, not for its relief."[4]

The first of these programs, the Public Works of Art Project (PWAP) was established in late 1933. The artists chosen for the PWAP received wages to create art work for public buildings supported by federal, state or local taxes. Artists were encouraged (although not required) to use local history and culture as their themes. Edward Bruce, a lawyer, businessman and amateur artist, was asked to join the Treasury Department to become the head of this new agency. Edward Rowan was his assistant while Forbes Watson, an art critic for the New York World, agreed to serve as the artistic director.[5] The PWAP was funded by a larger New Deal agency, the Civil Works Administration, which oversaw a wide variety of relief efforts. With a total national funding of one million dollars, it would exist for only six months. The PWAP paid weekly wages for up to two months of work. The wages of $25.50 to $42.50 per week were equivalent to those of skilled laborers. Employment under the Public Works of Art Project was not based in any assessment of artistic ability. Its primary purpose was to provide employment for artists as quickly as possible although Bruce and Watson attempted to consider artistic quality wherever possible in hiring. The program was implemented as speedily as possible. During the first four months of 1934, the period when the program existed, some 3,749 artists across the United States produced approximately 15,663 paintings, murals, and sculptures for government buildings, schools, and other public spaces. Dr. John Ankeney, director of the Dallas Museum of Fine Arts, became the head of Region 12 of the PWAP, which included Texas and Oklahoma.[6]

Assisted by a volunteer advisory board which included James Chillman of the Houston Museum of Fine Arts and Professor Florian Kleinschmidt of Texas Technological College, Ankeney chose artists as rapidly as he could, assigning them jobs in a variety of public buildings. Texas artists began to receive their PWAP commissions in December of 1933. Many of them executed murals because that constituted a preference on Ankeney's part. Since the project was conceptualized as a relief program, Dr. Ankeney had to limit his selections only to artists who could show financial need. Those individuals who were amateurs, or who were employed or had other financial resources, could not participate. Nonetheless he recruited almost one hundred artists in Texas alone, most of whom were at work within a month or so of the project's implementation.[7]

Although the agency's leadership was dominated by men, about one-fourth of the artists selected nation-wide were women. In Texas, female artists participated in larger numbers, especially in Houston where James Chillman advocated for them despite the gender prejudices of the era which favored men who, as heads of households, were presumed to need relief work to a greater extent than women. Chillman understood that women artists and art activists had been the moving force behind the promotion of the visual arts and the founding of the art museum in Houston. For that reason, since he largely controlled the PWAP commissions in Houston, Chillman assigned projects to both married and unmarried female artists. He justified these decisions to Regional Director John Ankeney in Dallas by noting women artists could paint strong and successful murals as well as their male counterparts. In fact, by the end of the project in the late spring of 1934, Chillman rated the work of many female artists as being of higher quality than the men.[8]

The statutory ending of the Public Works of Art Project in the late spring of 1934 did not stop all Federal funding for artists in Texas. As this agency came to end, the Federal government authorized the assignment of artists to camps of the Civilian Conservation Corps. Artists joined the CCC under similar conditions to other volunteers. They received room and board; medical care and clothing; lived at the camps in the same accommodations as other volunteers; ate army food; were subject to the same rules of military discipline as the other recruits; and were paid the same $30.00 per month. However, instead of doing manual labor the artists would make paintings and drawings of the men and their work at the camp. Because CCC artists had to purchase all their art supplies from their monthly salary, they tended as a group to do much of their work in pencil and crayon to save money. Only one hundred artists were authorized for the CCC camps but at least three Texans - Don Brown, William Lester and Douthitt Wilson – were enrolled in the program. This art would be government property and sent to Washington D.C. to document the work of the CCC.[9] In late 1934, Edward Rowan, the Treasury official in charge of the CCC artists, collected art from across the nation for a special exhibition in in Washington D.C. When this show at the National Museum ended First Lady Eleanor Roosevelt chose 26 works to display at the White House. At least one work by a Texas artist, Don Brown's drawing "Portrait," was among them.[10]

The PWAP and the CCC served as a proving ground for a larger Federal art program, the Section of Painting and Sculpture (also known as the Section of Fine Arts or The Section) of the Treasury Department. That department, at the time, superintended the construction of all public buildings belonging to the Federal Government. A new departmental policy required that one percent of the construction cost of any building had to be allocated for the creation of art work to embellish the building. Unlike the PWAP, commissions from the Treasury Department would be granted through competitions and based on merit rather than need. In Texas most of the commissions went for decorating post offices. Starting almost immediately, the New Deal embarked on a concerted effort of building post offices across the country, a program under the direction of Louis A. Simon, the Supervising Architect of the Treasury Department. Simon adopted a basic block design for post offices in smaller towns which followed a similar floor plan and had the same exterior dimensions throughout the country, although regional themes could be employed in modest architectural embellishments from place to place. Edward Bruce, who had previously directed the Public Works of Art Project, took charge nationally of the Section of Painting and Sculpture which commissioned the Post Office art projects. Most of this work in Texas took the form of murals although some artists, including sculptor Allie Tennant at Electra, executed bas reliefs. In all, artists decorated sixty-nine Post Offices across the state.[11]

These post office commissions were spread fairly evenly around the state with big cities such as San Antonio receiving large murals, in that case a series of historical scenes by Howard Cook. Post offices in smaller towns such as Goose Creek, Anson, and Seymour were granted smaller Section murals. Department policy required each artist to visit the town in which the mural would be placed to learn about its history, local culture, and civic attributes so the content of the piece would reflect some sort of specific local attribute. Almost all of these Post Office murals manifested an artistic style known as "American Scene," which involved a very realistic presentation of the subject as representational illustration, done in bright colors, and a content subject matter which reflected a positive view of American life and values with an emphasis on regional distinctions.[12] In addition to post offices, the Section of Painting and Sculpture also commissioned murals for new federal buildings in large cities like Amarillo, El Paso, Fort Worth and Houston.

Texas benefited from an additional source of federal funding not seen in other states during the New Deal namely, support for the celebration of the Texas Centennial of 1936. Although much of the funding for the Texas Centennial came from state monies expended from Austin, the Roosevelt administration provided significant amounts of financial support for these efforts through funding from a little-known New Deal agency, the United States Centennial Commission. This federal commission's only purpose was to help underwrite the costs of the celebration in Texas. As part of this celebration, a considerable number of activities, building projects, placement of historical markers, erection of statues, and the construction of two centennial fairs served to employ hundreds of artists, especially painters and sculptors. Artists found employment in the design, decoration, and embellishment of buildings, monuments, historical markers, and other structures commemorating Texas independence. That was the case because the design norms of the 1930s placed much emphasis on what was popularly known as "architectural art" which valued the incorporation of sculptural adornments, mural paintings, bas reliefs, carvings, artistic iron work, and tiles produced by visual artists in cooperation with architects.[13]

Texas centennial art funded by the New Deal appeared all over the Lone Star state, but especially in Fort Worth and Dallas where formal centennial celebrations took place in expositions similar to a "world's fair." In Dallas planners completely revamped the existing State Fairgrounds into the site of what became known as the Central Centennial Celebration. Hundreds of planners, artists, architects, and construction workers began laboring in 1935 to transform that east Dallas location into the site of an exposition boasting almost fifty new exhibit halls, pavilions, memorial structures, and esplanades. Fifty-one principle artists, painters, and sculptors executed murals, bas-reliefs, statues, friezes, metalwork and paintings as decorations for the new buildings, walkways, and water courses at Fair Park.[14]

In the early planning stages, some Texas artists complained the larger commissions at Fair Park went to out-of-state artists, but in the end most Texans who wanted employment received jobs, although sometimes as assistants to major artists from elsewhere. The Central Centennial Exposition at Fair Park also championed the cause of Texas art in general because the Dallas Museum of Fine Arts, located in one of the new buildings erected for the celebration, sponsored an art exhibit which highlighted artists from across the state. This centennial art show constituted perhaps the largest exhibit of Texas art ever assembled up to that time.[15] In all, the exhibition presented work from 164 Texas and southwestern painters, etchers and sculptors.[16] Thanks to the effort of Fort Worth booster Amon Carter, that city also sponsored a large centennial celebration. Located on land at the western edge of the city, the Frontier Centennial Exposition resulted in the construction of numerous buildings including a theater, a coliseum, show barns, and entertainment venues, many of which artists decorated in themes celebrating the history of Texas. Most notably, artist Kenneth Gale produced a massive ceramic mural on the main façade of the Will Rogers Coliseum which to this day remains an artistic landmark in Fort Worth.[17]

However, neither Dallas' Central Centennial Exposition nor Fort Worth's Frontier Exposition acknowledged the participation of minorities in Texas. African American leaders sought Federal help to remedy this. Under heavy pressure from the Federal level and the Dallas Negro Chamber of Commerce supported by other black civic groups, the local organizers of the Central Centennial Exposition in Dallas agreed to spend $50,000 of Federal money to build the Hall of Negro Life at Fair Park and another $50,000 to fund its exhibits. This focus on African Americans was "a first for any World's Fair."[18] A major exhibition of nationally recognized African American artists (including Aaron Douglas, Palmer Hayden, and Archibald Motley) was mounted in the Hall of Negro Life. In addition to the work of professionals, artwork by school children was shown. Two Texas artists, Samuel Albert Countee of Houston and Frank Sheinall of Galveston, were included in the show. Texas artists exhibited in the Hall of Negro Life at the Centennial State Fair were selected from the annual Allied Arts Exhibit organized by Dallas's Federation of Colored Women's Clubs.[19]

During the Centennial, the State of Texas also embarked on an ambitious program of erecting statues and bas reliefs of individuals prominent in the history of the settlement of the province in the 1820s and the Texas Revolution In the end, state funding could not underwrite this entire program. Money from the United States Centennial Commission was therefore earmarked for its costs. Once this program was placed under the auspices of the Federal Government, former Texas Governor Pat Neff headed a committee to select sculptors to create these statues. A. Webb Roberts, a Dallas businessman knowledgeable of such matters as a long-time granite dealer, superintended the Markers and Memorial Program, as it become known. Although it began in 1936, it took several years for all of the statues, twenty in number, to be placed at locations around the state. In addition to marking several hundred historical sites with granite memorials, Roberts contracted with various artists to craft bas-relief panels of an historical nature on courthouse lawns.[20]

Taken in its entirely, the amount of Federal government support for the visual arts in Texas was not a large sum of money when compared to other projects and programs in the state. However, it proved to have a profound impact on invigorating the development of artistic activities, especially in furthering the popularity of the "American Scene" as an *au-courant* artistic style. These programs, especially the PWAP and the post office murals commissioned by the Treasury Department, provided needed work for artists who suffered financially in the 1930s, as did Americans from all walks of life. Importantly, Federal support for the arts in Texas during the New Deal created an enduring, living legacy of public art, much of which can still be seen across the Lone Star State.

Notes and Acknowledgments

[1] Ann Prentice Wagner, *1934: A New Deal for Artists* (Washington, D. C.: The Smithsonian Institution, 2009), 19-28; Richard D. McKinzie, *The New Deal for Artists* (Princeton: Princeton University Press, 1973). Nick Taylor, *American Made: The Enduring Legacy of the WPA, When FDR Put the Nation to Work* (New York: Bantam, 2008), 270-71.

[2] Kenneth B. Ragsdale, *Centennial '36: The Year America Discovered Texas*, (College Station: Texas A&M University Press, 1987). Light Townsend Cummins, "History, Memory, and Rebranding Texas as Western for the 1936 Centennial," in *This Corner of Canaan: Essays on Texas in Honor of Randolph B. Campbell*, ed. by Richard B. McCaslin, et. al., (Denton: University of North Texas Press): 37-57.

[3] Biddle, a member of a wealthy East Coast family, had Texas connections which routinely brought him to Dallas. in the decades after World War I. He had married the granddaughter of Col. A. H. Belo, the founder of the Dallas Morning News. As such, Biddle owned stock in the newspaper. He regularly visited Dallas in the 1920s and 1930s on Belo family business. This put him in contact with the fledgling arts community in the city, especially artists belonging to the Dallas Art Association and the Highland Park Society of the Arts. Ralph Purcell, *Government and Art: A Study of the American Experience* (Washington, D.C.: Public Affairs Press, 1956), 47-50. Quotations from Biddle and Roosevelt come from Biddle's autobiography: George Biddle, *An American Artist's Story* (Boston: Little, Brown and Company, 1939), 268-69.

[4] Henry Morgenthau, Jr. Interview, November 9, 1964 in Archives of American Art, quoted in Roger Kennedy, *When Art Worked: The New Deal, Art, and Democracy* (New York: Rizzoli, 2009), 38.

[5] Lenore Clark, *Forbes Watson: Independent Revolutionary* (Kent, OH: Kent State University Press, 2001), 104-06.

[6] Victoria H. Cummins, "Prejudice and Pride: Women Artists and the Public Works of Art Projects in East Texas, 1933-1934," *East Texas Historical Journal*, Vol. 53, No. 2 (Fall 2015): 88-114.

[7] V. Cummins, "Prejudice and Pride;" 96 Texas artists are listed in PWAP records, 33 of them women. Statistics compiled by Victoria Cummins from various PWAP records.

[8] V. Cummins; "Prejudice and Pride;" James Chillman, Jr. to John S. Ankeney, March 28, 1934, with attached clipping, NARA RG 121, AAA roll DC-13.

[9] William Lester, Interviewed by Sarah Hunter, May 29, 1984, *Dallas Historical Society Archives*, Hall of State, Dallas, Texas; "Extracts from a letter received from J. Douthitt Wilson, Artist at E.C.W. Camp SP-14, Canyon, Randall County,

Texas," n.d., National Archives and Records Administration (NARA) RG 121, Microfilm by the Smithsonian Archives of American Art (AAA), roll DC-1; Clipping, "Marshall Artist Sketching at CCC East Texas Camp," N.p., n.d., *Don Brown Scrapbook* Volume II, Harrison County Historical Museum, Inez Hartley Hughes Research Library, Marshall, Texas; Letter, W. Frank Persons to State CCC Agencies, September 14, 1934, General Correspondence of the Division of Selection 1933-42, NARA RG 35 Entry 36, Box 3.

[10] Letter, Edward B. Rowan, Director, Section of Painting and Sculpture, to Don Brown, October 30, 1934, Correspondence with and about Artists in the Civilian Conservation Corps Camps 1934-37, NARA, RG 121, Entry 142, Box 1. Clipping, "Don Brown Work in White House. Local Artist's Work Selected by Mrs. Roosevelt for Exhibit," N.p., n.d., Don Brown Scrapbook Volume II; "CCC Workers' Art to Hang in Capitol," *New York Times* 16 June 1935.

[11] Phillip Parisi, *The Texas Post Office Murals: Art for the People* (College Station: Texas A&M University Press, 2004); Robert L. Stevens and Jared A. Fogel, "Conflict and Consensus: New Deal Mural Post Office Art," *National Social Science Journal*, Vol. 13, No. 2 (January 2010): 160-66; Bryan E. Wheeler, "From Coit Tower to College Station: Radical Artists and the Texas Post Office Murals," paper presented at the Texas New Deal Symposium Fort Worth Texas, June 14, 2014; Bryan E. Wheeler, "Oh Pioneers! Peter Hurd's Big Spring Post Office Mural in Context," paper presented at the West Texas Historical Association, Odessa, Texas, April 4, 2014.

[12] Erica Doss, "Coming Home to the American Scene," in Jason Schoen, et. al., *Coming Home: American Paintings 1930-1950* from the Schoen Collection (Athens, Ga.: Georgia Museum of Art, the University of Georgia, 2003), 28-29. Matthew Baigell, *The American Scene: American Painting of the 1930s* (New York: Praeger, 1974), 13.

[13] William H. Wilson, *The City Beautiful* (Baltimore: Johns Hopkins University Press, 1989), 254-280.

[14] "Lists of Artists at Fair Park," [1980] Miscellaneous Artist Folder, Artists and Architects Files, Centennial Collection, Dallas Historical Society, Dallas, Texas.

[15] There were centennial art exhibitions elsewhere across the state. The Houston Museum of Fine Art, for example, celebrated the anniversary with a much smaller exhibit that included the museum's purchase prize acquisitions in Texas art, along with the Will C. Hogg's collection of Frederick Remington works.

[16] Exhibition of Paintings, Sculpture, and Graphic Arts, June 6 to November 29, 1936 (Dallas: Texas Centennial Exposition, Department of Fine Arts, 1936), 68-91 in the collection of the Texas/Dallas History and Archives Division, Dallas Public Library.

[17] "Frontier Exposition to be Opened by Roosevelt," Fort Worth Star Telegram, July 19, 1936. Jan Jones, Billy Rose Presents Casa Manana (Fort Worth: TCU Press, 1999). Jacob Olmstead, "From Old South to Modern West: Fort Worth's Celebration of the Texas State Centennial and the Shaping of an Urban Identity and Image," (PhD Dissertation, TCU, 2011).

[18] Paul N. Dunbar, "A. Maceo Smith and the Hall of Negro Life," *Legacies: A History Journal for Dallas and North Central Texas* 23 (Fall 2011): 4–12.

[19] "Negro Women's Clubs Plan Art Exhibition." *Dallas Morning News*, June 28, 1936.

[20] Lana Henderson, *Leaving a Track: A Biography of A. Webb Roberts* (Dallas: The Baptist Foundation of Texas, 1985); Harold Schoen, comp., Monuments Erected by the State of Texas to Commemorate the Centenary of Texas Independence (Austin: Commission for Control for Texas Centennial Celebration, 1938.); Light Townsend Cummins, "Statues of the State," *The Medallion* (July-August, 2011), 6-9.

South Texans in Washington During the New Deal

George M. Cooper

As former Texas State Historian Light Cummins has noted when speaking about the built environment of Texas in the New Deal era, "... academic historians have not much studied these aspects of the New Deal in a systematic manner."[1] The same can be said about those denizens of Washington, D.C. who hailed from South Texas during the Administration of Franklin Delano Roosevelt. With the exception of Lionel V. Patenaude's *Texans, Politics and the New Deal*, most historians of the New Deal have focused on Roosevelt and his coterie in the Executive Department with little attention to state personalities or issues. That is changing, especially with regard to Texas. Historians such as Keith Volanto, Michael Botson, Bernadette Pruitt and Cynthia Brandimarte have published books dealing at least in part with various aspects of the Great Depression and the New Deal. But, with the exception of Steven Feinberg's Unprecedented Power: Jesse Jones, Capitalism, and the Common Good, and the first volume of Robert Caro's multiple volume biography of Lyndon Johnson, little has been done in the field of Texans who played a role in the New Deal in Washington, even less has been done on the New Deal in South Texas.[2] This article will start the discussion of South Texans who played a role in Washington during the New Deal Era.

Three groups of Texans served in Washington during the period in question. There was some degree of overlap as there always is in Washington. South Texans were found in all of them. First, of course, the Executive Department, which included John Nance Garner, a man described by Raymond Clapper, the United Press reporter who coined the term "smoke filled rooms," as displaying "complacent country sagacity," and historian Dixon Wecter as "a political wiseacre."[3] Garner of course was responsible for the original appointment of Jesse Jones, the most important, and certainly the most powerful, Texan in Washington during the Roosevelt era, to the Board of the Reconstruction Finance Corporation by President Herbert Hoover. Second, the Congress, which included not only the members of the Senate and House, but also Garner in his role as President of the Senate, and former Speaker of the House. And finally, a group that has not received enough attention, Texans who were neither elected officials nor members of the executive branch yet played a role either as an appointee or lobbyists. Included in the latter group were businessmen with strong Texas ties, such as Ralph W. Morrison of San Antonio and William L. Clayton of Clayton, Anderson and Company, and the former Mayor of Corpus Christi, Roy Miller.[4]

Since the Civil War Texas, essentially, has been a one-party state. With a few exceptions no Democrat has been elected to any state-wide elected office since Ann Richards left the Governor's office. Throughout the New Deal era Texas was a one-party state dominated by Democrats. It was not merely partisan bluster when Congressman J. J. Mansfield of Columbus told the *Victoria Advocate* on March 6, 1931 that "During the long years he has been in public life . . . he has never seen such unmistakable evidence of a Democratic trend throughout the nation . . ."[5] Little did he realize that the last Republican Congressman from Texas to hold office prior to the election of 1932, Harry M. Wurzbach of Seguin, would die six months later on November 6, 1931. That same day the papers announced Wurzbach's death and simultaneously announced that the inevitable election of a Democrat to fill his seat from the 14th District of Texas would throw the majority in the House of Representatives to the Democrats.[6] With the election of Richard M. Kleberg, Sr. of Kingsville, that prediction was fulfilled. And while Kleberg was a Democrat and Wurzbach was a Republican, by marriage they are considered to be part of the same extended political dynasty in the United States Congress.

The members of the Texas Congressional delegation during the New Deal era were primarily conservative in nature, both fiscally and socially. Many were, in the words of Thomas L. Stokes, " . . . by in large the chosen of the dominant social and economic interests."[7] Patenaude argues that J. J. Mansfield, Richard Kleberg, and Garner's successor Milton O. West, were never "New Dealers."[8] Dig into the morass of the New Deal and you will find that their support for the New Deal programs came from the partisan concept that these programs originated in a Democratic administration. In addition, the opportunity to obtain federal dollars for their districts motivated many of the Texas delegation. That opportunity was demonstrated by the $1,476,000 loan to Eagle Pass in John Nance Garner's 15th Congressional District for the construction of an irrigation canal announced on November 1, 1932 by the Reconstruction Finance Corporation, just days before the presidential election.[9] However, some Texans, especially old-line Populist oriented Democrats such as Texan Sam Rayburn, occasionally thought proposed New Deal legislation did not go far enough.

Thomas L. Stokes in his 1940 memoir stated, "American politics had undergone a transformation . . . The middle class no longer dominated the nation's life or its policies."[10] Many within the Democratic Party wanted to focus of what Roosevelt called "the forgotten man at the bottom of the economic pyramid" which included many in the agrarian sector as well as the urban working class. Stokes argued that the Republicans of 1936 did not realize the change had occurred, but the same can also be said the many of the Texas Congressional Caucus. One Texan who apparently did not realize this change had occurred was Richard Kleberg, Sr. of the 14th Congressional District. He was important because when elected to replace Harry Wurzbach in 1931 he gave the Democrats control of the House of Representatives during the election year of 1932. His election also made it possible for John Nance Garner to be elevated to the Speakership.[11] Kleberg spent his entire congressional career on the House Agriculture Committee, and sponsored the bill creating the Farm Credit Administration in 1933.[12] Still, Kleberg often showed his conservatism when New Deal Legislation was up for a vote. Although an attorney by education, he was primarily known as a rancher who certainly was aligned with the 1932 Democratic platform which promised to control crop surpluses and remove government from all fields of private enterprise except where necessary to develop public works and natural resources in the common interest. Although aware of the needs of the agricultural sector of the economy, originally he was opposed to the Agricultural Adjustment Act, stating that it was "radical and socialistic." Kleberg was ultimately convinced to vote for the bill by Lyndon B. Johnson, whom he had hired as his Congressional Secretary, and the lobbyist, former Mayor of Corpus Christi, and head of the 1932 Texas Roosevelt campaign committee, Henry Pomeroy "Roy" Miller.[13]

Johnson certainly realized that a transformation in the political focus of Washington had occurred, and Miller probably did as well. According to Mary Jo O'Rear, author of two books dealing with Corpus Christi during the New Deal Era, some felt that Kleberg had a somewhat unimpressive character. Yet, despite his unobtrusive personality, after his conversion on the question of the Agricultural Adjustment Act, PWA money was used to create the Port in Brownsville, in the southern portion of his district. Of course, it didn't hurt that the Chairman of the House Committee on Rivers and Harbors was the aforementioned J. J. Mansfield of Columbus, another South Texas Congressman. In addition, through the hard work of Lyndon Johnson, Kleberg's 14th Congressional district had one of the highest number of Civilian Conservation

Corp camps in the entire country and was the only district to have one hundred percent of its Agricultural Adjustment Administration loan applications approved.[14]

Monetary policy was one of the key issues addressed in the Agricultural Adjustment Act. Many within the agricultural sector of the economy favored a pro-inflationary policy as a method of alleviating the debt of the farmer. Passage of the Agricultural Adjustment Act, which included sweeping monetary changes, exposed the contrary economic interests within the Texas delegation. Some such as Texas Congressman Martin Dies favored action "to do something about silver," but other such as Texas Senator Thomas Connally favored general devaluation to solve monetary problems on a broader scale.[15] While lawyers like Connally favored devaluation, bankers, such as Vice-President John Nance Garner, greatly resented much of what ended up in the final Agricultural Adjustment Act because it reduced the interest they earned on farm loans from fourteen percent to five, costing them a substantial amount of revenue.[16] Even before his nomination for Vice-President, Garner, a banker, had demanded federal loans for the needy.[17] Nonetheless, his hostile attitude towards individuals such as Henry Morgenthau evidenced an animosity towards the Farm Credit Act and Emergency Mortgage Credit Act that would lead later to his opposition to Roosevelt's third campaign. It does not appear, however, Garner extended his ill feelings towards Richard Kleberg who had sponsored the Farm Credit Act in the House of Representatives.

While most of the "Texas Gang" sprang from the conservative side of the Democratic Party, the election of 1934 brought a maverick within the Texas Democratic Caucus. Maury Maverick was another who realized there had been a change in the American political system. He was elected with the aid of Lyndon Baines Johnson whom Maverick recruited away from the staff of Richard Kleberg after San Antonio was removed from Kleberg's district and the 20th Congressional District was created.[18] Maverick, the most "liberal" member of the Texas delegation, challenged and beat the "City Machine" which ran San Antonio. Despite the "City Machine's" close affiliation with John Nance Garner, Garner arranged financing of Maverick's 1936 re-election campaign at Roosevelt's request.[19] Further, Maverick was one of the southern "liberals" in Congress who spoke on behalf of improving the lot of African Americans, so it was no surprise when he was "primaried," out of office in a very close race in the 1938 Democratic primary, and served only two terms. Roosevelt withheld his endorsement of Maverick until just before departing the state from Lubbock on his 1938 primary swing through Texas.[20] Many felt that that had Roosevelt endorsed him while in Central Texas, Maverick probably would have won. However, Roosevelt was more focused on purging those conservative Democrats he believed disloyal rather than helping liberal supporters who he thought would be re-elected without trouble. Roosevelt's focus on the purge cost him several liberal supporters including Maury Maverick.[21]

While serving in Congress, Maverick was seen by the Roosevelt administration as one of the more responsible members of the 1934 class of "New Deal Democrats." Support for the administration proved beneficial as during his second term funds from the United State Housing Authority were approved for the removal of the Mexican American "corrals" in San Antonio well ahead of urban renewal projects in larger cities. He later would be elected Mayor of San Antonio, and it was during his term as Mayor that the WPA funding was approved for the construction of the San Antonio River Walk. Still Maverick took issue with some members of the administration. Arthur M. Schlesinger, Jr. reported Maverick shouting at Rexford Tugwell about an Agricultural bill proposed by Tugwell because the language used by Tugwell to explain his proposal was beyond the comprehension not just the American public but also beyond that of himself and other members of Congress.[22]

The domestic banking crises which the country suffered through was only a part of a much larger problem. The international banking system was also in total disarray. Chaos reigned throughout the industrialized world as countries tried to stabilize their currency and simultaneously stabilize international exchange rates. A conservative government in France vehemently argued for a return to the gold standard and deflation. Another conservative government in Great Britain abandoned the gold standard and pushed inflationary concepts, feverishly arguing that the United States should do the same. As the European industrialized powers pushed for a grand international economic conference, Roosevelt refused to commit to either view. In early June of 1933, Roosevelt named the members of the United States delegation to the London Economic Conference. It was headed by the Secretary of State, Cordell Hull, an odd choice because he was primarily interested in trade rather than monetary policy. Most of the remaining members of the delegation reflected the eastern orientation of the New Deal. But there were exceptions. Roosevelt chose his 1920 running mate, Senator James Cox of Ohio; as well as Senator Key Pittman from Nevada, the Chairman of the Senate Foreign Relations Committee and Congressman Samuel

D McReynolds of Tennessee, Chairman of the House Foreign Affairs Committee. Also included was Ralph W. Morrison of San Antonio who was primarily known as a fund raiser for the Texas Democratic Party and friend of John Nance Garner.[23]

Morrison, one of the founding members of the South Texas Chamber of Commerce in 1926, was head of the Pan-American Hotel Company and one-time owner of the St. Anthony Hotel in San Antonio. He would also be named to serve on the Federal Reserve Board on February 10, 1936 by Roosevelt, but he resigned from that position just five months later on July 9th. A native of Missouri, Morrison began his career as a foreign automobile sales manager with the St. Louis Car Company. He also worked in the utilities industry until 1925 then moved into investments, ranching and banking in Texas until 1934. Later he would serve as the President of the Texas-Mexican Railway company and organized the Central Power & Light Company. In his will, Morrison bequeathed the income from a trust he created to Baylor University which the university used for its law school.[24]

The commission with Morrison, Hull, Cox, Pittman, and McReynolds departed for London and what was supposed to be a monetary stabilization conference turned chaotic even before the party arrived in London, in no small part because Roosevelt took the United States off the gold standard while they were enroute. Once they arrived, Hull presented his proposals for a ten percent reduction of international trade tariffs; Pittman was an advocate of silver, and when it became obvious that he would not get his way, he drank and quarreled with everyone. McReynolds and Morrison apparently gave up in disgust and rarely attended any of the sessions.[25]

Morrison's sponsor, John Nance Garner, had gone to Congress as a Jeffersonian, trust-busting, anti-Wall Street, Populist oriented Progressive. That form of progressivism quickly devolved into conservatism in the face of the problems of the Great Depression for which they had no answer. Garner, in fact, had gone so far as to argue for an Ogden Mills designed, Hoover sponsored, tax increase in order to balance the budget during the last year of the Hoover administration. Later that year, at the Democratic National Convention, while standing third in the number of votes for the nomination behind Roosevelt and the 1928 nominee, Al Smith, as the southern "conservative" candidate, Garner ended as Roosevelt's vice-presidential nominee in return for putting Roosevelt over the top. A pragmatic politician, Garner promised passage of a "beer bill," to help alleviate the Republican deficit in the post-election rump session just after to the 1932 election.²⁶ Garner would leave Washington eight years later as an avid conservative who frequently used his experience to secretly manipulate the opposition to Roosevelt's programs in both the House and the Senate.²⁷

Garner's dislike of the Farm Credit Act and the Emergency Mortgage Credit Act were not the only times when his views would clash with those of the president. When the investigation into the banking practices of J. P. Morgan and his affiliates revealed that several conservative Democrats, including William H. Woodin, Roosevelt's original Secretary of Treasury, had been on Morgan's "Preferred List" of individuals, a split occurred within the cabinet. In 1929, those on the "Preferred List" had purchased shares of Standard Brands at $20.00 a share, while market value was between $31.00 and $35.00. The profit to these individuals was substantial when they sold their shares. Several cabinet members, led by Garner, thought that these individuals should be fired, or at least resign, from their government positions. Roosevelt disagreed, making the statement that several people had done things in 1929 that they probably would not do in 1933.²⁸

In late 1936, following the sit-down strikes organized by the CIO for higher wages for all unskilled industrial workers, Roosevelt's allies proposed the Fair Labor Standards Act. It would raise the minimum wage to forty cents an hour, at a time when Garner was paying the Mexican pecan pickers on his farm one cent per pound, or $1.00 per day on a good day, and his carpenters in his Uvalde home building operations twenty-five cents an hour. The Act was passed in 1938, but with major carve outs and exceptions which assured that it would not apply to agricultural workers, and other rather disenfranchised groups, to placate southern Democrats, including Garner.²⁹

By 1937, the President and his Vice-President were at loggerheads over several issues. Roosevelt's support of labor legislation was a sticking point with Garner. On April 1 of that year, Senator James F. Burns of South Carolina offered an amendment to the Guffey-Snyder Coal Act which would prove to be a combustion point between the two. The Act itself was an attempt on behalf of labor to navigate around the Supreme Court decision striking down the NRA. The Burns amendment would condemn sit-down strikes, which had proved successful in organizing the auto industry, in the mines. Ultimately the disagreement between Roosevelt and Garner over Garner's support of the Burns Amendment led to a shouting match between the two at a White House meeting.³⁰ Added to the ongoing dispute over the court packing plan, the rift between the Roosevelt progressive wing of the party, and the Garner conservative wing of the party developed into a large chasm. Garner would once again toy with the idea of running for the Presidency in 1940.

Ultimately Garner and most of the Texas delegation broke with Roosevelt over the issue of the Court Packing Plan. Hatton Summers of Dallas refused to permit the House bill out of committee forcing Roosevelt to rely on the Senate for initial passage. Since Democrats and Independent Progressives dominated the Senate with only twenty-two Republicans holding seats in 1937, merely holding his party together meant success for the President. All Republicans were opposed to the plan. The Independent Progressives were open to discussion, but generally considered to be opposed to it. The leader of the Progressive Democrats in the Senate, Burton Wheeler of Montana was opposed to it. The matter would eventually depend on the conservative Southern Democrats. The best indication of what was to come occurred when Vice-President Garner left Washington for his home in Texas in mid-June before the issue came to a vote in the Senate, indicating his disapproval. Garner also must have realized that the court had already become more compliant when it upheld the revised Frazier-Lemke Act, known as the *Farm Mortgage Moratorium Act, in Wright v Vinton Branch of Mountain Trust Bank of Roanoke* on March 29, 1937.[31]

Although generally considered to be conservatives, John Nance Garner, Richard Kleberg, Sr., and J. J. Mansfield all played important roles in the passage of New Deal legislation. All helped pass New Deal legislation that they felt ran against the interests of Texas business and businessmen. Maury Maverick was an unrepentant liberal which ultimately lead to his defeat by the conservative forces that controlled the San Antonio political scene. Lyndon Johnson would quickly take up Maverick's mantle in Congress. Other Texas members of the Congress drifted away from the Roosevelt administration programs after the court packing plan. Other Texans in Washington also waxed and waned as programs and people they championed drew political attention, but for a brief period, the South Texas Democrats in Washington had been among the most important group in the city and nation. Still more work needs to be done to bring the role played by the individuals to the public's attention.

Notes and Acknowledgments

[1] Cummins, Light Townsend, "With Stone, Canvas and Mortar: When Art and Architecture Went to Work for the New Deal in Texas," paper presented at the Texas New Deal Symposium, Greenville, Texas, June 15, 2013.

[2] Pautenaude, Lionel V., *Texans, Politics and the New Deal*, (New York: Garland Publishing Inc., 1933); Volanto, Keith J., *Texas, Cotton and the New Deal*, (College Station: Texas A&M University Press, 2005); Botson, Michael R., Jr. *Labor, Civil Rights, and the Hughes Tool Company*, (College Station: Texas A&M University Press, 2005); Pruitt, Bernadette X. *The Other Great Migration: The Movement of Rural African Americans to Houston, 1900 – 1941*, (College Station: Texas A & M University Press, 2013); Brandimarte, Cynthia A., *Texas State Parks and the CCC*, (College Station: Texas A & M University Press, 2013); Feinberg, Steven. U*nprecedented Power: Jesse Jones, Capitalism and the Common Good.* (College Station: Texas A & M University Press, 2011); Caro, Robert A. *The Years of Lyndon Johnson: The Path to Power* (New York: Alfred A. Knopf, 1982).

[3] Schlesinger, Arthur M., Jr. *The Age of Roosevelt, Vol. II: The Coming of the New Deal* (Boston: Houghton Mifflin Company, 1959), p. 425; Wecter, Dixon. *The Age of the Great Depression, 1929 – 1941*, (New York: The MacMillan Company, 1948), p. 48.

[4] Schlesinger, p. 141

[5] *Victoria Advocate*, March 6, 1930

[6] *The Evening Independent*, St. Petersburg, Florida, November 6, 1931, p. 1 (http://www.google.com/newspapers?nid=ivNPAAAAIBAJ8sjid=11QDAAAA-IBAJ8pg=1655,34946878) (accessed Dec. 23, 2013), The *Sun Journal*, Lewiston, Maine, November 6, 1931 (http://Google.com/newspapers?nid=-19138dat=193111-68id=1_goAAAAIBAJ8pg=3986,3086385) (accessed Dec. 23, 2013)

[7] Stokes, Thomas L, *Chip off my Shoulder*, (Princeton University Press, 1940), p. 529

[8] Pautenaude, op. 75

[9] *Victoria Advocate*, November 1, 1932, p. 1

[10] Stokes, p.529

[11] Wecter, p. 52; Caro, p. 220; Stokes., p. 421

[12] "Caesar Kleberg Wildlife Research Institute – Named Endowments," (http://www.ckwri.tamuk.edu) accessed 04/16/2014;

[13] Caro, pp. 213 – 214; "The Governorship," The *Victoria Advocate*, Nov. 7, 1932, p. 1

[14] O'Rear, Mary Jo Holoubeck. *Storm Over the Bay: The People of Corpus Christi and their Port* (College Station: Texas A&M University Press, 2009); *Bulwark*

Against the Bay: The People of Corpus Christi and their Seawall (College Station: Texas A&M University Press, 2017); Personal correspondence in possession of the author, December 5, 2013; Schlesinger, p. 288; "Notable Tribute is Paid Mansfield by His Colleagues," *Victoria Advocate*, February 16, 1941, p. 1, 2.

[15] Caro, p. 260

[16] Schlesinger, p. 211

[17] Ibid, 426 - 427

[18] Caro, p. 260.

[19] Wecter, p.53

[20] Caro, p. 558

[21] Wecter, p. 165; Stokes, p. 494 – 495

[22] Stokes, p. 507; Caro, p. 276; Wecter. p.128; Schlesinger, p. 534.

[23] Schlesinger, p. 208

[24] "South Texas Chamber of Commerce," *Handbook of Texas Online* (http://www.tshaonline.org/handbook/online/articles/das01), accessed April 20, 2014. Uploaded on June 15, 2010.; (Walkerreport.blogspot.com/2007/really-short-history-of-st-anthony-hotel.htm) accessed 11/07/1023; (www.federalreserve.gov/bios/boardmembership.htm) accessed 11/07/2013; "The Federal Reserve Service, 100 Years – Ralph W. Morrison," (www.federalreservehistory.org/People/DetailView/88) accessed 04/09/2014; "About Baylor Law" (http://www.baylor.edu/law/about/index.php?id=76318) accessed 04/12/2014

[25] Schlesinger, p. 205-206.

[26] Schlesinger, 211; Hamby, Alonzo L. *For the Survival of Democracy: Franklin Roosevelt and the World Crises of the 1930s,* (New York: Free Press, 2004), p. 139 – 140; 90; *Victoria Advocate*, November 4, 1932, p. 2.

[27] Stokes, p. 507.

[28] Stokes., pp. 436 – 437; Caro, p. 558; Korstad, Robert Rogers, *Civil Rights Unionism: Tobacco Workers and the Struggle for Democracy in the Mid-Twentieth Century South* (The University of North Carolina Press, 2003) p. 132.

[30] Hamby, p. 349.

[31] 300 U.S. 440 (1937).

Eleanor Roosevelt and a Woman's New Deal in Texas

Mary L. Scheer

In 1938 Mrs. S. E. Boone and I. M. Howard, two black women desperate for work, penned a letter to Eleanor Roosevelt. Despite months of trying to get relief from the Works Progress Administration (WPA) officials in San Antonio, they turned to the first lady to protest their treatment. Black women, they complained, were treated "very bad at the WPA offices." They could only qualify for "the most menial jobs, such as maids, charwomen and the like." They could never be clerical workers or sales women. While there were jobs for whites and Mexican women, blacks were often refused or "so abused that they could hardly stay on the job." "Work and food," they pleaded, "are what we are asking for, for our children."[1]

The source of Boone and Howard's frustration began with the stock market crash on October 24, 1929, plunging Texas and the American economy into a tailspin. Massive unemployment became the most visible symbol of the deepening Depression. Nationally, in March 1933, 12.6 million workers, or about one quarter of the work force, were out of work. In Texas estimates placed the number between 350,000 and 400,000. Of those unemployed, Texas ranked eighth in the nation with 105,045 families or 7.1 percent of the population on relief. The next year there were 246,819 cases, or 13 percent of the population. Almost five years later when Boone and Howard wrote their letter, unemployment remained at an unacceptable 14 percent.[2]

Although Texans did not immediately feel the full effects of the downturn, the faltering economy and its devastating consequences eventually reached every city, farm, and region. Initially, many Texans subscribed to the proclamation by President Herbert Hoover that "prosperity was just around the corner." Local relief agencies and limited federal assistance, he assured the nation, would alleviate the worst effects of the Depression. While citizens at first demonstrated a considerable amount of optimism, recovery was stubbornly slow as the nation and state faced the greatest economic crisis ever known.

The Great Depression profoundly affected most Texans but took its greatest toll on women. Like Boone and Howard, Texas women viewed the hard times through the lens of their families' wellbeing. Providing adequate food, shelter, and clothing for their children was a priority, particularly when their husbands were out of work or simply left home, abandoning their families to fend for themselves. Married women who held jobs before the crash were routinely fired in favor of male heads of household. Prevailing gender roles dictated that men were breadwinners with dependents while women were homemakers who should not compete with men for scarce jobs. While federal relief policy from the outset provided that "needy women shall be given equal consideration with needy men," in practice, many positions were reserved for men only. If women were offered work, it was in lower paid, less prestigious jobs traditionally related to "women's work," such as sewing, canning, and child care.[3]

During the 1930s Texas was still a rural state with many women living on cotton farms or ranches and laboring in traditional spheres of work. They had narrow choices centered around housework and fieldwork with "limited social networks" to escape their daily chores. When cotton prices fell from 10 cents to 5.3 cents a pound in the fall of 1931, farm families began to feel keenly the effects of the Depression. While Texas farmers reacted to falling prices by taking almost 6 million acres out of production, farm women survived by practicing "ruthless under-consumption," and doing without all but basic needs. Eleanor Roosevelt, observing the day-to-day lives of women during the decade, commented: "It means endless little economies and constant anxiety for fear of some catastrophe...."[4]

The Depression accelerated urbanization of the state as many Texas women, especially young unmarried girls, moved from the farms to the cities. They migrated for various reasons, mainly tied to the economic decline in rural areas. Many came in search of wage-paying jobs, as farm families typically sent their "eldest daughter into the city to work, often as a domestic servant." Others arrived seeking to escape the monotony and isolation of farm life. And still others came in search of a husband and a chance to set up their own household. Some girls, however, were forced to return to rural life because hard times made jobs scarce in cities as well. Nevertheless, those that stayed included many of the approximately half a million Texas women working for wages in the 1930s, officially pushing the majority of the state's population into urban areas by 1940.[5]

As the economy continued to free fall, "Depression-weary Texans" and other Americans were ready for a change. On the national level, Franklin D. Roosevelt campaigned for the presidency in 1932 and famously spoke of the "forgotten man at the bottom of the economic pyramid." Both his optimistic words and later bold presidential actions under the New Deal helped restore a measure of public confidence. At the state level, Miriam "Ma" Ferguson, the first female governor of the state, won a second term (1933-1934) that corresponded to Roosevelt's first two years in office. Although previous charges of corruption and political interference by husband and former governor "Farmer Jim" Ferguson plagued her administration, she campaigned on cutting taxes and reducing appropriations to address the state's pressing financial crisis.[6]

While most state actions in the emergency originated from Washington, D.C., Governor Ferguson utilized her office to try and deal with the worsening Depression. To stem the fear and hysteria of runs on banks, she declared a bank moratorium. She then confronted the state debt, estimated at approximately $14 million, and reversed her campaign stand on reducing taxes by proposing both state sales and corporate income taxes. Ferguson also supported many New Deal initiatives, including federal oil price controls and "Bread Bonds" for state work relief. Most importantly, when funds became available to Texas from the federal government, Ferguson established the Texas Relief Commission to secure jobs for unemployed Texans. With the passage of the Federal Emergency Relief Act (FERA) in May 1933, an even greater financial windfall befell the Ferguson machine, igniting political fighting in Austin and renewing charges of corruption and "outright fraud."[7]

With a woman in the Texas state house, some reformers assumed that Ferguson's victory represented the advancement and acceptance of women in the public sphere. But Miriam Ferguson was no feminist or supporter of the recently won right to vote for women. When she issued the executive order creating the Texas Relief Commission, she held traditional beliefs concerning well-established gender roles. Since her marriage to James Ferguson in 1899, she was a devoted wife and mother who left "control of the family finances solely under her husband's direction." As governor she had little political experience and generally deferred to her husband, who made many of the decisions. As she remarked in a 1914 interview: "For myself, I have led such a sheltered life and such a contented life, that I have really given little thought to the subject of women's suffrage. My husband has always attended to every business care. I have never had to feel the responsibility of any of that sort of thing, and even if I had the right to vote, I do not think that I would care to use the right." If Ferguson acknowledged the plight of women during the Depression, it was to rally their support to clear her husband's name, rather than assist them in securing jobs, especially those traditionally held by men.⁸

In contrast, Eleanor Roosevelt was a highly-visible first lady who worked tirelessly for the inclusion of "the forgotten woman" in New Deal relief programs. A political cartoon published in the *Dallas Morning News* in 1938 titled "Giving her a lift to town" depicted the first lady driving a car and offering assistance to a jobless woman. Known through her newspaper column, "My Day," numerous magazine articles, and fact-finding trips, Eleanor encouraged frustrated Americans to correspond with her directly. And they did, amounting to 300,000 letters in 1933 alone. Unconstrained by an official position within the administration and with access to New Deal administrators and the president, she became an intermediary between the average citizen and the government. One San Antonio mother laid off from federal employment wrote the first lady that "in September when school starts it will be impossible for mine to attend, they will have no shoes & there [sic] clothing is no better than rags." Another unemployed woman wrote her that she had "four little children depending on me." She had no money, no home, and no milk for her three-month-old baby. Even young girls wrote letters, such as a ten-year-old child from Brownsville, asking for "a few toys for me and my little sisters" for Christmas.⁹

As an advocate for social and economic justice, Eleanor Roosevelt called attention to the thousands of homeless, unemployable women during the Depression. In a 1933 book titled *It's Up to the Women*, she rejected societal norms that dictated woman's place was in the private sphere of the home, and that "she must marry, and if she did not marry, she had no work in the world." Like Meridel Le Sueur in *Women on the Breadlines*, she understood that women "suffered more quietly than men." They did not sell apples or beg on street corners but wandered the alleys "invisible" to passersby and neglected by federal relief agencies. Instead of despair, Roosevelt believed that modern women wanted to be "able to do something which expresses her own personality even though she may be a wife and mother." In September 1933, she therefore vowed to "get something done" for the women.¹⁰

One of the earliest work relief federal programs was the Civilian Conservation Corps (CCC), signed into law March 31, 1933. But it was officially limited to young unmarried males between the ages of seventeen and twenty-five years. Combining education and recreation with outdoor life and work, CCC camps employed more than half a million young men to work on reforestation projects, building bridges, and combating soil erosion. While Eleanor applauded these efforts and helped establish lending libraries for the camps, she also crusaded for similar programs for needy young women. Enlisting the aid of Secretary of Labor Frances Perkins, she argued that over half of the underprivileged youth of the nation were women, who also needed immediate assistance.[11]

On June 10, 1933, FERA opened the first experimental camp for women in upstate New York. Modeled on CCC camps--but with important differences--critics sneeringly referred to them as "She, She, She" camps. Few in number, the women's camps were primarily run by the states with FERA grants. Rather than plant trees or build bridges, they would receive experience in communal, democratic living, instruction in hygiene and nutrition, and recreational activities. Whereas the young CCC men worked generally for a year and received wages, the women received emergency assistance, but only "small allowances" for two or three months.[12]

Dismayed by a lack of an official New Deal for women, Roosevelt sponsored a White House Conference on the Emergency Needs of Women on November 20, 1933. She sought the help of Harry Hopkins, FERA director; Molly Dewson, Director of the Women's Division of the Democratic Party; Ellen Sullivan Woodward, recently-appointed FERA head of the Women's Division and approximately fifty prominent women from around the country. She opened the conference by stating: "As a group, women have been neglected in comparison with others, and throughout this Depression have had the hardest time of all." In his keynote address, Hopkins estimated that "over 400,000 women required immediate help," while "only fifty thousand women were actually on relief." Part of the difficulty, he said, was the prevailing notion that women were too weak to work outdoors and those with families could not easily travel and would require jobs near their local communities.[13]

To break the bureaucratic and cultural resistance to establish more women's camps, Roosevelt crusaded for an enlarged "parallel camp" program for needy young women aged twenty to twenty-five years. She offered to host a second White House Conference on Camps for Unemployed Women. On April 30, 1934, approximately 75 people, mostly women, met in the nation's capital and developed a new plan of action. Hopkins quickly endorsed the project and informed relief administrators in Texas and elsewhere of the availability of limited funds. Once again, Eleanor's intercession gave important support to the program and federal funding for 90 such schools and camps for women nationwide.[14]

Along with letters and site visits, first-hand information about how ordinary Texans experienced the Depression reached Eleanor Roosevelt through her friend and rumored intimate, Lorena "Hick" Hickok. A former veteran AP reporter, Hickok had accepted a field investigative position with FERA from Harry Hopkins, to "go out around the country and look this thing over." He told her: I don't want statistics from you. I don't want the social-worker angle. I just want your own reaction, as an ordinary citizen." Viewing the crisis up close, Hick would later write over 100 reports to Hopkins, as well as numerous letters to Eleanor, documenting the suffering and despair of the American people. From January 1933 to August 1934, Hick traveled the country by car and proved to be a keen observer of New Deal efforts to solve the Great Depression.[15]

On one such investigative trip, Hickok covered in two weeks over two thousand miles of Texas roads in her "secondhand Chevrolet convertible, christened Bluette." Setting out from Washington D.C. on March 25, 1934, she arrived in Houston seventeen days later. She interviewed businessmen, blue- and white-collar workers, farmers, social workers and "unemployables"—those unskilled and undereducated. Hick characterized the state as "a Godawful mess." She reported that the weekly food allowance for single women in Houston had been reduced to 39 cents. Federal relief reached 12,500 families and 2,700 single men and women, with new applications pouring in at a rate of 1,100 a week. Further, the state legislature and the governor's office were in a political battle concerning alleged graft and the selling of state relief jobs.[16]

As Hick crisscrossed the sprawling state, she visited numerous Texas towns and cities. Her reports revealed a mixture of both misery and hope. San Antonio was "feeling an improvement" due to the presence of the US Army and the goat raising industry, which were key sectors of its economy. In Dallas the Lone Star Gas Company sales "climbed to a three-year high." But in El Paso five banks had failed, and its silver and copper industries were struggling. While the lumber industry was depressed, oil, cotton, and grain exports in the Port Arthur-Beaumont region "appeared to be in good shape." Construction starts were slowing in Houston, but jobs in the oil fields were available. However, petroleum companies, she complained, let orders go unfilled rather than give jobs to unskilled workers, preferring to hire workers with specialized skills. Disgusted by their lack of New Deal spirit, she contemptibly wrote: "Those babies are [only] thinking in terms of 1929 profit." Worse yet, Texas businessmen routinely scorned the National Recovery Administration (NRA) codes, taking advantage of "government priming" and suspension of anti-trust laws.[17]

Hickok also called attention to the largely invisible problem of out-of-work Texas women, particularly young single girls. They included "the middle-class, often college-educated girls," as well as "women adrift, anonymous, without work or family." Although homeless and hungry, they rarely appeared on the breadlines and escaped the attention of most relief agencies. There were no "flop houses," work relief, or food programs for them. Some resorted to prostitution such as a Houston woman who desperately solicited a customer that "It only costs a dime." Hick reported the plight of this overlooked group to Hopkins who pledged to "find jobs for these women where they now are and get them to work with as little delay as possible."[18]

Along with reports and correspondence from Hick, Eleanor Roosevelt also traveled the country to investigate first-hand the crippling economic conditions and report on New Deal programs. In 1933 she traveled to the mining areas in West Virginia. There Eleanor noticed whole families living in worn out tents or company houses "scarcely fit for human habitation." Women and children suffered the most, she observed, with little food, virulent diseases, and scant medical care. As was her practice, when she returned to the White House Eleanor met with her husband for an uninterrupted meal so that he could hear the entire story "not dulled by repetition."[19]

As a result of her frequent trips to depressed mining areas, Eleanor Roosevelt pitched "the homestead idea," to Franklin Roosevelt. Known as the Subsistence Homestead Division (SHD) under the Department of the Interior, it was a New Deal agency that provided homes to the urban poor and a plot of land on which to grow crops for home consumption, not commercial sale. At the same time, the program required part-time employment by a family member, providing additional cash income from an outside source. Eleanor described the project as "experimental work," designed to get people off relief, put them to work, and give them enough land to start growing their own food during the Depression. The president concurred with Eleanor's vision as he too believed that homesteading in a rural environment offered "dignity and comfort" to the poor rather than the crowded cities.[20]

4.1 Eleanor Roosevelt visiting WPA nursery school for black children, 1936.

Courtesy Franklin D. Roosevelt Presidential Library.

The first subsistence homestead community was Arthurdale near Morgantown, West Virginia. But there were also over 30 others across the country, including five in Texas. Those in the Lone Star State were Beauxart Gardens in Jefferson County, Houston Gardens in Houston, Three Rivers Gardens in Three Rivers, Wichita Gardens in Wichita Falls, and Dalworthington Gardens in Tarrant County. Eleanor Roosevelt originally suggested the site at Dalworthington Gardens near Fort Worth where she often visited family members nearby. Most homestead communities were short term experiments, lasting until the late 1930s, providing modest track housing for families and three and one-half acres of land. Residents continued to hold part-time jobs in industry or at the oil refineries while farming the land. For many Depression-era women and children the homestead program provided their first real home, a sense of community, and hope for rising standards of living.[21]

Along with the urban poor Eleanor Roosevelt was deeply troubled by the plight of the nation's youth. She worried that American youth, faced with long term unemployment, would lose faith in democracy. "I live in real terror when I think we may be losing this generation," she stated in May 1934. Earlier, FERA had created resident centers, shelters, and work camps for transient youth with supplementary resident camps for young women. These camps offered women training in home economics, health care, creative arts and hairstyling. But these early efforts were never sufficient to assist "the hundreds of thousands of disadvantaged youths." With the support of Hopkins and Aubrey Williams, his assistant administrator, Eleanor urged a broader plan to a reluctant president--one that would "help high school and college youngsters finish school and provide training in both resident and nonresident projects." She waited until her usual time for discussing such questions with the president—just before he went to sleep. Soon thereafter, on June 26, 1935, the National Youth Administration (NYA), her "pet project" came into existence.[22]

One of the more successful NYA programs was in Texas, directed by twenty-six-year-old Lyndon B. Johnson. It was composed of both "in school" and "out of school" jobs on resident and non-resident projects. One of the earliest programs Johnson initiated was a work program to keep high school and college students enrolled through paid work on their campuses. Students performed varied tasks as clerks or maintenance workers. Wages ranged from an average of $6 a month for high school students, $15 for college students, and $20 for graduate students. More than 18,000 "boys and girls" were able to continue their education and another 10,000 received part-time employment. Hearing of the good work out of the Austin office, Eleanor frequently "dropped in" to see for herself "the new training program."[23]

Since the state was still largely rural with towns a far distance apart, NYA resident or "live in" projects involved agricultural-related skills. Most projects were located on nearby college campuses where unemployed young farm women attended classes in marketing, canning, and sewing clothing to be distributed to local relief agencies. The first resident training project in Texas was located at Prairie View State Normal and Industrial College. W.R. Banks, principal of the college, planned the program with NYA officials "to train young black women for domestic service, using instructors and facilities at the college." However, the first enrollees came from urban areas, rather than rural settings, where domestic job opportunities were more plentiful. But later college officials began selecting girls from rural regions as well, where they could utilize their acquired skills in smaller towns and communities. For example, 30 girls from coastal counties resided at Blinn College as part of a stenographic and clerical program. Girls in Giddings received instruction in home economics and household duties for two weeks then off for two weeks, receiving $18 pay. And 26 girls enrolled in a NYA recreational leadership program in San Marcos. Other NYA locations were added at Texas A&M College, Texas Tech College, and North Texas Agricultural College.[24]

Lyndon Johnson and his successor Jesse Kellam also set up three additional camps for underprivileged young women at Glen Rose, Houston and San Antonio. The camps offered classes in "English, home economics, civics and typing," as well as providing recreational activities such as swimming, hiking, and baseball. At one Texas camp women even defied accepted stereotypes and undertook "the more rugged work of building vacation cottages." In spite of the success of the experimental women's camps, in 1937 Congress closed them down as part of an austerity program to cut "expensive New Deal social programs." Hilda Worthington Smith at the national NYA office complained: "As so often the case, the boys get the breaks, the girls are neglected."[25]

Non-resident projects were also employed statewide to aid needy young women. Under the direction of Ellen Sullivan Woodward, director of the Women's and Professional Projects, the NYA, as well as the WPA, placed women in traditional jobs as seamstresses, school cafeteria workers, clerks, domestic servants, nurses' aides, and playground assistants. One of the most common relief projects for women was sewing rooms, which "enjoyed uncommon success" throughout the state. In San Antonio, Anglo and Mexican-American women dominated in the sewing rooms, while in Dallas and elsewhere black women were segregated toward domestic service. Eleanor Roosevelt frequently toured these facilities, confessing that her visits had become "somewhat automatic." One NYA official declared that the projects for girls were "not on a par with those for boys, most of them being of the sewing-room variety." Nevertheless, by August 1936 approximately 1,800 girls were employed in NYA sewing rooms across Texas.[26]

Ellen Woodward, now a WPA official, also headed the New Deal Arts Section known as Federal Project One. Enthusiastically supported by Eleanor Roosevelt, the WPA program supported unemployed actors, musicians, writers, and artists. Although small, the Texas Theater Project (FTP) operated in Dallas, Fort Worth, San Antonio, and Houston, where Margo Jones was FTP assistant director and founder of the Houston Community players. Lucille M. Lyons of Fort Worth directed the Texas Music Project, centered in San Antonio, Fort Worth, Dallas, and El Paso.

4.2 Beatrice Denmark inspecting a NYA sewing room in San Antonio, predominated by Mexican American women, February 1937. San Antonio Light Collection, University of Texas Institute of Texan Cultures, San Antonio, Texas.

This program provided work to approximately 200 professional musicians, mostly men on relief; however, unemployed female music teachers received jobs teaching music and others participated in federally-sponsored programs, featuring Mexican songs and music, as well as symphony concerts. When the project was revamped in 1939, the Music Project continued under the sponsorship of the Texas State College for Women until early 1942. The Writers' Project employed out-of-work writers and emphasized the American Guide series on the history and culture of various states. Published in 1940, the Texas Guide included "twenty-one essays on various aspects of Texas society, profiles of fifteen cities, and twenty-nine tours." Another significant project was the gathering of ex-slave narratives by WPA writers. Over 300 original interviews were collected from former Texas slaves living during the Great Depression, of which 128 were females. Former slaves Lucy Lewis and Ellen Payne both remembered slavery as not as harsh as the Depression years, recalling that "there was always plenty to eat." The federal government also supported artistic endeavors through the Art Project. Originally created in 1933 as a relief program under the Public Works of Art Project (PWAP), it later evolved to providing commissions for "embellishment of public buildings." Texas artists such as sculptors Allie Tennant and Waldine Tauch who sculpted the Tejas Warrior and Moses Austin respectively for the 1936 Texas Centennial celebration, and post office muralist Suzanne Scheuer, were women who benefited from New Deal federal arts funding.[27]

Even during the waning years of the Depression, Eleanor Roosevelt continued to undertake frequent trips around the country, giving paid lectures, inspecting New Deal programs, and talking to ordinary men and women. A March 1939 three-week train trip through the South and into Texas was fairly typical. After riding the rails through Virginia, Tennessee, Mississippi, and Louisiana, she crossed the Sabine River at Deweyville and proceeded to Beaumont, College Station, Sherman, Abilene, Waco, Houston, Edinburg, San Antonio, and far West Texas, exiting into New Mexico. All along the way she toured New Deal programs that addressed the plight of the American people, especially the "forgotten woman." She inspected NYA training programs in Beaumont, "practice houses" for rural girls in Hillsboro, a medical work program for girls at Jefferson Davis Hospital in Houston, a rural school in Cypress, the needlework industry in San Antonio for female workers, and other WPA projects. When she returned to the White House, she provided either written or oral reports to the president and other agency heads.[28]

Born in the era of gender inequality and Jim Crow laws, Eleanor Roosevelt was well aware that New Deal relief programs were often discriminatory. The Federal Economy Act of 1932 barred the government from employing both husband and wife from a single-family unit. This law disproportionately affected married women who were routinely fired from jobs since the WPA allowed only one job per destitute family, presumed to be allotted to the male head of household. Single, divorced, and widowed women fared a bit better since the category of heads of household included single persons, with or without dependent children. While work relief programs (with the exception of the CCC) were officially available to both men and women gender bias excluded women from construction and other outside jobs, channeling them into stereotypical, lower paid jobs.[29]

Racial discrimination and workplace stratification by sex also disadvantaged African American women in securing federal work relief. New Deal programs regularly upheld and reinforced the segregation laws of the South. In urban settings such as Houston, the monthly WPA relief benefits for blacks averaged $12.67, while whites received $16.86. In rural areas black women, living as tenants or sharecroppers, were frequently thrown off the land, ineligible for many farm programs. The Women's and Professional Division in Texas contributed to the inequality by "professionalizing homemaking," thereby defining suitable work for black women as employment in lower paid domestic work. At the same time NRA minimum wage laws and other standards did not always apply to black women who were concentrated in jobs in private homes, hotels, or laundries. Lula Gordon, a black Texas woman, wrote Eleanor Roosevelt that "black women were forced into accepting domestic jobs though such work often proved of short duration." As historian Merline Pitre observed, the majority of black Texas women were fixed in domestic servant occupations, which "imprisoned them at the bottom of the economic ladder."[30]

Mexican-American women fared better than blacks in securing federal jobs. However, in San Antonio, separate relief projects were maintained for the races and caseworkers channeled Mexican-American women into lower-paid work, reserving white-collar positions for Anglos. A few women such as Manuela Gonzalez found work as a library aide in a Cotulla school, but "most Tejanas were sent to poorly equipped and segregated training sites." Others were relegated to canning and sewing rooms. Furthermore, those Hispanic women who were neither American-born or naturalized citizens, were often denied relief and employment due to their alien status.[31]

As she traveled the country as her husband's "eyes, ears, and legs," Eleanor Roosevelt confronted examples of racism, segregation, and social injustice. She was always disturbed by the conditions blacks, Hispanics, and the poor endured. But she was also aware of the fragile social and political relations in the South, which prevented her husband from challenging the southern leadership of his party. As the president explained, he would risk being pushed out of office, along with his New Deal initiatives to end the Depression. Nevertheless, Eleanor continued to speak out in favor of the NAACP, anti-lynching laws, desegregation, and equality for the sexes. In Texas and elsewhere, she opposed the Klan, segregation in homestead communities, and later (1954) efforts by White Citizens' Councils to block desegregation efforts. She also worked to create employment for jobless women and achieve equity for those on relief. While she was instrumental in securing some gains for women and minorities in the 1930s, her considerable influence, however, did not overturn traditional racial and sexual stereotypes in society and the workplace.

Despite tremendous pressures that discouraged the hiring of women in Depression-era Texas, wage-earning women made significant strides toward creating a Woman's New Deal in the state. During the 1930s women either "made do" to compensate for reduced income or worked outside the home in greater numbers, many in federal relief programs. However, New Deal agencies often reinforced job segregation by sex and assigned lower pay scales for women. In addition, half of the work force—clerical workers, domestic servants, and farm women—were left out of New Deal opportunities. In frustration, many women wrote Eleanor Roosevelt to complain about their unequal treatment. An advocate for women and minorities, she was sympathetic to the plight of the "forgotten woman." Possessed with power, prestige, and access, Eleanor Roosevelt traveled the country during the Depression, connecting the public to the government and ensuring that New Deal relief agencies served the most destitute and neglected groups. She increased awareness of women's needs, helped shape New Deal policies toward women, aided thousands of women and youth in gaining marketable skills and educational assistance, and prodded New Deal administers, including her husband, to provide fair treatment and access to relief programs. Further, she directly championed the creation of women's camps, subsistence homesteads, youth programs, and a host of other relief projects that assisted women and families. Without her advocacy on behalf of women, a Woman's New Deal would have looked very different for Texas and the nation.[32]

Notes and Acknowledgments

[1] The Works Progress Administration became the Work Projects Administration in 1939. Ruthe Winegarten, *Black Texas Women: A Sourcebook* (Austin: University of Texas Press, 1996), 175-176; Judith N. McArthur and Harold L. Smith, *Texas Through Women's Eyes: The Twentieth Century Experience* (Austin: University of Texas Press, 2010), 88.

[2] FERA Unemployment Relief Census, Oct. 1933, Report One, 4; Susan Ware, *Beyond Suffrage: Women in the New Deal* (Cambridge: Harvard University Press), 1981), 106-107; Rupert N. Richardson, et. al., *Texas: The Lone Star State*, 10th ed. (Boston: Prentice Hall, 2010), 326.

[3] Ware, *Beyond Suffrage*, 106-107.

[4] Eleanor Roosevelt, *It's Up to the Women* (n.p.: Frederick A. Stokes, 1933); 8; McArthur and Smith, Texas Through Women's Eyes 61; Rebecca Sharpless, "Women and Work during the Great Depression" in *Invisible Texans: Women and Minorities in Texas History*, Donald Willett & Stephen Curley, eds. (Boston: McGraw Hill, 2005), 144-155ff. See also Jeane Westin, *Making Do: How Women Survived the '30s* (Chicago: Follett, 1976).

[5] Susan Ware, *Holding Their Own: American Women in the 1930s* (Boston: Twayne Publishers, 1982), 10-11; Sharpless, "Women and Work during the Great Depression," 151.

[6] Carol O'Keefe Wilson, in *The Governor's Shadow: The True Story of Ma and Pa Ferguson* (Denton: University of North Texas Press, 2014), 188; McArthur and Smith, Texas Through Women's Eyes, 68-69. See also The American Presidency Project, Radio Address, April 7, 1932, www.presidency.ucsb.edu.

[7] Ron Tyler, ed., *The New Handbook of Texas*, "Great Depression" (Austin: Texas State Historical Association, 1996): 3:301-309; Tyler, ed., *The New Handbook of Texas*, "Miriam Amanda Ferguson," 2: 981-982; Wilson, *In the Governor's Shadow*, 195-196; Harry Hopkins, *Spending to Save: The Complete Story of Relief* (Seattle University of Washington Press,1936), 95-107ff; Richard Lowitt and Maurine Beasley, eds., *One Third of the Nation: Lorena Hickok Reports on the Great Depression* (Urbana: University of Illinois Press, 1981), 216.

[8] Wilson, *In the Governor's Shadow*, xv; El Paso Herald, August 11, 1914.

[9] Political cartoon, *Dallas Morning News*, November 22, 1938; Records of the WPA, files 661& 662, National Archives, Washington D. C.; Julia Kirk Blackwelder, *Women of the Depression: Caste and Culture in San Antonio, 1929-1939* (College Station: Texas A&M University Press, 1984), 60; *Dallas Morning News*, November 22, 1933; Cathy D. Knepper, ed., *Dear Mrs. Roosevelt: Letters to Eleanor Roosevelt Through Depression and War* (New York: Carroll & Graf Publishers, 2004), 118. See also http://www.firstladies.org/biographies.

[10] Roosevelt, *It's Up to the Women*, 143-145, 142-152ff, 166-167; Blanche Wiesen Cook, *Eleanor Roosevelt, 1933-1938* (New York: Viking, 1999), 2:74, 86; Michael Golay, *America 1933: The Great Depression, Lorena Hickok, Eleanor Roosevelt and the Shaping of the New Deal* (New York: Free Press, 2013), 190. See also Meridel Le Sueur, *Women on the Breadlines* (New York: West End Books, 1977).

[11] Adam Cohen, *Nothing to Fear* (New York: Penguin Books, 2009), 225-289; Carol A. Weisenberger, D*ollars and Dreams: The National Youth Administration in Texas* (New York: Peter Land, 1994), 19.

[12] Cook, *Eleanor Roosevelt*, 2: 88-90; Ware, *Beyond Suffrage*, 111-112.

[13] Cook, *Eleanor Roosevelt*, 2:86; *New York Times*, Nov 20, 1933; Ware, *Beyond Suffrage*, 106-107. See also FERA Unemployment Relief Census, Oct.1933.

[14] Ware, *Beyond Suffrage*, 112-115; Cook, *Eleanor Roosevelt*, 2:88.

[15] Hickok to Eleanor Roosevelt, April 11, 19, 20, 1934, *Hickok Papers*, FDR Library, Hyde Park, New York; Hickok to Hopkins, April 11, 13, 17, 1934, *Hopkins Papers*, FDR Library; Lowitt and Beasley, eds., *One Third of the Nation, ix;* Golay, *America 1933*, 39, 190.

[16] Hickok to Hopkins, April 11, 1934, in Lowitt and Beasley, eds., *One Third of the Nation*, 216; *Golay, America*, 1933, 91, 236-239.

[17] Hickok to Hopkins, April 11, 1934, in Lowitt and Beasley, eds., *One Third of the Nation*, 217; *Golay, America*, 1933, 236-239.

[18] *Golay, America 1933*, 133-134,190; *Le Sueur, Women on the Breadlines*, 1, 5; *Hickok to Hopkins*, April 13, 1934, in Lowitt and Beasley, eds., *One Third of a Nation*, 222-223.

[19] Roosevelt, *This I Remember*, 177-180; Cook, *Eleanor Roosevelt*, 2:133-134.

[20] Roosevelt, *This I Remember*, 178.

[21] The name of Dalworthington Gardens is the combined names of Dallas, Fort Worth, and Arlington. It still exists today. Roosevelt, *This I Remember*, 179.

[22] See National Youth Administration, Boxes 73, file NYA-Appointment & other Correspondence; 28, file NYA, Lyndon B. Johnson Presidential Library, Austin, Texas (hereafter referred to as LBJPL). Eleanor Roosevelt, *Autobiography* (New York: Harper & Brothers, 1937), 192-193; NY Times, May 7, 1934; Weisenberger, *Dollars and Dreams*, 20.

[23] T. H. Watkins, *The Great Depression: America in the 1930s* (Boston: Little, Brown, and Co., 1993), 258-259; Tyler, ed., *The New Handbook of Texas*, "National Youth Administration," 4:950; White House Famous Names, Box 9, folder "Mrs. Eleanor Roosevelt," NYA Papers, LBJPL; Eleanor Roosevelt to Lyndon Johnson, June 17, 1941, NYA Papers, box 9, folder "Roosevelt family, LBJPL; Joe T. Cook, et. al. to Richard R. Brown, resolution, April 24, 1937, NYA Papers, Box 73, folder: Appointments & Other Correspondence.

[24] Wiesenberger, *Dollars and Dreams*, 84-86; *Austin Statesman*, December 9, 1938; *Giddings News*, October 21, 1938; *Austin American*, June 18, 1938.

[25] "Girls Broken by Depression Get Grip on Life," *Ft. Worth Star Telegram*, Sept. 27, 1935, 4; Weisenberger, *Dollars and Dreams*, 144-145.

[26] Weisenberger, *Dollars and Dreams*, 144; Blackwelder, *Women of the Depression*, 111, 118; *Dallas News*, August 13, 1938; Austin American November 18, 1938; Michael Barr, "A Comparative Examination of Federal Work Relief in Fredericksburg and Gillespie County," *Southwestern Historical Quarterly* Vol. XCVI, No. 3 (January 1993): 375; Ware, *Beyond Suffrage*, 108-110.

[27] Richard R. Brown to LBJ, March 31, 1936, NYA Papers, LBJPL; Roger Biles, *The South and the New Deal* (Lexington: University Press of Kentucky, 1994), 77-79; Kenneth E. Hendrickson, Jr. "The WPA Arts Projects in Texas," *East Texas Historical Journal* Vol. XXVI, No. 2 (1988): 3-11; Jerre Margione, *The Dream and the Deal: The Federal Writers' Project, 1935-1943* (Boston: Little, Brown and Co., 1972), 263-265; Light Cummins, *Allie Victoria Tennant and the Visual Arts in Dallas* (College Station: Texas A&M University Press, 2015), 107-109; 120-121,139; Philip Parisi, *The Texas Post Office Murals: Art for the People* (College Station: Texas A&M University Press, 2003), 47; Tyler, ed., *The New Handbook of Texas*, "Theater," 6:456; Ware, *Beyond Suffrage*, 109-110; Richard D. McKinzie, *The New Deal for Artists* (Princeton, N.J.: Princeton University Press, 1973), 82-83, 158-159; Ronnie C. Tyler & Lawrence R. Murphy, *The Slave Narratives of Texas* (Austin: Encino Press, 1974), 57; Ronald E. Goodwin, *Remembering the Days of Sorrow: The WPA and the Texas Slave Narratives* (Buffalo Gap: State House Press, 2013), 78.

[28] Eleanor Roosevelt, "My Day," Feb 27-March 20, 1939; Mary L. Scheer, "Bound for Beaumont: Eleanor Roosevelt's 1939 Train Trip through East Texas and Beyond," *East Texas Historical Journal* Vol. 54, No. 2 (fall 2016): 7-21.

[29] McArthur and Smith, *Texas Through Women's Eyes*, 88; Blackwelder, *Women in the Depression*, 69.

[30] Ruthe Winegarten, *Black Texas Women: 150 Years of Trial and Triumph* (Austin: University of Texas Press, 1995), 179-180; Merline Pitre "At the Crossroads: Black Texas Women, 1930-1954 in *Black Women in Texas History*, Bruce A. Glasrud and Merline Pitre, eds. (College Station: Texas A&M University Press, 2008), 29; Biles, *The South and the New Deal*, 56.

[31] Teresa Paloma Acosta and Ruthe Winegarten, *Las Tejanas: 30 Years of History* (Austin: University of Texas Press, 103; Blackwelder, *Women in the Depression*, 60-74, 109-129; McArthur and Smith, *Texas Through Women's Eyes*, 88.

[32] See Westin, *Making Do*.

"The Yield on this Investment Should be High"
National Youth Administration:
A Texas Experience

Carroll Scogin-Brincefield

I have determined that we shall do something for the Nation's unemployed youth because we can ill afford to lose the skill and energy of these young men and women. . . In recognition of this great national need, I have established a National Youth Administration, to be under the Works Progress Administration. It is my sincere hope that all public and private agencies, groups and organizations, as well as educators, recreational leaders, employers, and labor leaders will cooperate whole-heartedly with the National and State Youth Administrations in the furtherance of this National Youth Program. The yield on this investment should be high.[1]

The National Youth Administration (NYA), a New Deal agency, was announced by President Franklin D. Roosevelt on June 26, 1935. It was originally a component of the Works Progress Administration (WPA), headed by Harry L. Hopkins. In 1939, following passage of the Reorganization Act, the NYA was transferred into the Federal Security Agency. Then, shortly after the start of World War II, the NYA was put under the War Manpower Commission WMC). The NYA was headed by Aubrey W. Williams, a prominent liberal from Alabama who was close to Harry Hopkins and Eleanor Roosevelt. The head of the Texas division at one point was Lyndon B. Johnson (1935-1937), followed by Jesse Kellam (1937-1943). The program benefited over 280,000 Texas youths and 4,800,000 young people nationally. The NYA provided dollars for disadvantaged youths from 1935 to 1943,[2] and gave jobs to more than 600,000 college students and 1,500,000 high school pupils through its student aid program. "From the standpoint of cost, it was the cheapest work relief, combining part-time employment with little equipment and overhead at a yearly average of $225.00 apiece."[3] The federal government spent approximately $184,000,000 on the NYA between July 1935 and June

1939.⁴ This money was stretched to reach 5,000,000 young people and was used to finance an immense variety of jobs throughout the nation. The young men and women in the program, as well as the diverse activities in which they participated, presented an "excellent testimony"⁵ in the words of President Roosevelt and in the eyes of the nation.

The criticisms of the program should not be discounted, for there were genuine expressions of concern that the NYA might destroy the independence of American education.⁶ Another criticism came from conservatives who feared that the resident training centers and girls' camps were a "hotbed of Communism."⁷ Yet, the fears of the NYA critics were never substantiated. Among the most plausible criticisms of the NYA was the charge that many of the work projects were supervised by inexperienced local administrators and were underfinanced. However, even those who criticized the program usually concluded that "by holding back the torrent of unemployment and the prolonging of education through any means," youths were better equipped "for the economic struggle ahead."⁸ In April 1939, President Roosevelt publicly announced his own evaluation of the youth program by stating, "The NYA . . . has developed a program which has proven its effectiveness in meeting this need."⁹

To attempt an evaluation of a national program as diverse and decentralized as the National Youth Administration is not an easy task. The program consisted essentially of forty-eight state National Youth Administrations supervised by a Washington office. Each of the states' NYA directors established activities to fit the special needs of his state's youth. The problems of poverty and unemployment were shared, but a great amount of diversity existed in the way this recovery program was implemented in each state. The federal government appropriated the money for the youth project, but to comprehend the impact of the NYA, it should be examined on the state and local levels.

Thousands were on the state relief rolls in 1935, and Texas was ripe for the New Deal work programs. In August 1935, Lyndon Johnson estimated that his home state had more than "100,000 unemployed youths within our age limit on relief."¹⁰ Texas mirrored the national youth unemployment situation. The various programs of the Federal Emergency Relief Administration (FERA) and the Civilian Conservation Corps (CCC) left many young Texans needing jobs to finance their educations or simply to support themselves and their families.

One such young lady, 15-year-old Mattie Mae Pierson from rural Cuero in Dewitt County, came to San Antonio in March 1935; alone and in hopes of earning money for her family of six back in Cuero. She found a job at the Main Street Taxi Dance, where she made 3 cents for every dance and for every glass of beer that she induced a customer to buy. In a dance-floor fight between two customers, a gun went off and Mattie Mae was killed. The public outcry demanded the dance clubs be closed, but with no apparent results.[11]

5.1 Mattie Mae Pierson. Courtesy San Antonio Light Collection, University of Texas Institute of Texan Cultures, San Antonio, Texas

Many youth in need of assistance had dropped out of high school and college in the early years of the Depression, searching in vain for nonexistent jobs or for jobs that were unsafe (as with Mattie Mae). The state still had a predominantly rural economy, and the drought of the early 1930's and the resulting "dust bowl" added to the crises which had plagued the American farmer and forced many Texans into dire financial conditions. Johnson established state and local advisory committees to assist him in providing relief to the youth. Realizing that the national office could not develop nationwide work projects to meet the varying needs of youth across the country, Aubrey Williams considered these boards crucial in aiding state directors to find support, sponsors, and funding for NYA programs best suited to their districts, typifying the decentralized nature of the NYA. Johnson appointed prominent local citizens to approximately 200 community and county advisory committees. They worked with the NYA district directors to develop out of school work projects and to keep a "pulse" on the local economy, identifying areas of private employment that can offer opportunities for NYA trained youths in the future.[12]

State and local advisory committees of the NYA served as more than practical advisors. They exemplified the democratic character of the NYA and the New Deal in general. After assembling administrative staff, appointing the State Advisory Committee, and selecting district directors to work with local advisory boards throughout Texas, Johnson began to operate one of the outstanding NYA programs in the nation. Johnson won the admiration of the Washington office by faithfully and tirelessly adhering to the guidelines. At the meeting of the state directors in August 1935, Johnson learned that the state objectives of the NYA were designed to provide relief to needy youths through the student aid program and out of school work projects, to offer guidance and placement service, and to develop productive leisure time activities.

August 1935 was the most action-packed month of the Texas student aid program for decisions had to be made quickly if the program was to be in existence for the coming semester. September quickly approached; the student aid program received top priority and provided financial aid to needy youths between 16 and 24 years of age who could not continue their education without such assistance. This NYA program incorporated the student aid program for college students under the FERA and extended it to include students enrolled in elementary and high schools. The aid took the form of wages for part-time jobs rather than student loans. The program for high school students, known as the School Aid Program, was new. Johnson and H.A Ziegler, who oversaw the student aid in the early months, had to impress upon the high school officials the constraints of following procedures to ensure that their students were paid promptly by the NYA.[13] The decentralized nature of the NYA was again apparent in the student aid program. The NYA provided the funds and set the guidelines for the student aid program, but school administrators determined who would receive aid in the jobs the students would perform to earn NYA money. Texas authorities in 2,575 schools and 84 colleges and universities assigned part-time jobs based on need.

Originally, students receiving school aid, but not those receiving college aid, had to be from families on relief. The decision to make non-relief students eligible for school aid occurred in October 1935 with clear instructions that school officials were "to exercise every precaution to make certain that his funds were not made available to any student who did not produce satisfactory evidence that NYA employment was essential to the proper continuance of his education."[14] Some schools spent more time initiating projects that would provide marketable skills or complement the student's major interest. For example, in Lincoln School for African Americans in Dallas, Texas, NYA boys worked in the school's auto mechanic shop repairing and maintaining school vehicles under the supervision of the auto mechanics teacher. In a high school at Kenedy, Texas, 9 students learned woodworking skills as they planed, sanded, and refinished 200 badly battered old desks.

The superintendent of Fort Worth schools accepted the local group's suggestion that the NYA students be organized to assist the police department in directing traffic at heavily congested intersections around schools for an hour before and after classes. In Waco, Baylor University officials developed a project in which the Waco public school system employed 10 young men, most of whom were Sociology majors, to visit "the homes of the underprivileged children of school age who had been absent from school and who were maladjusted both in the home and in the school" in an effort to understand and reduce attendance problems. This project successfully decreased the truancy rate and was a valuable experience, complementing the students' classroom work in sociology.[15] Assigned to the biology department at North Texas State, a former participant remembered that the step-by-step procedure she followed for stuffing ducks. She prepared various species of ducks for study in the labs.[16] The diverse jobs exemplified the attempt made by school officials to avoid make work and to initiate a program of value to both the students and communities. The decentralized structure of the student aid program however meant that not all NYA students would benefit from the same quality projects as those provided by more innovative and concerned officials, as those in Waco, Fort Worth, and Denton.

The eight years of operation in the NYA's student aid program assisted 125,000 Texas high school students and 75,000 college students. Those in high school received a maximum of six dollars per month while the maximum for college and graduate students was twenty and thirty dollars respectfully. Over the years, actual wage averaged approximately $4.25 per month for high school students and $15 per month for college and graduate students. Many of the boys and girls in high school used their earnings for such necessities as carfare, school supplies, lunch money, and shoes. Some contributed their NYA dollars to the family income. One former participant who worked as a janitor's helper and clerk typist remembered her wages helped her mother feed, clothe, and educate their family of seven when her father abandoned them. Another recalled that she gave her monthly six dollars to her parents "to help buy sugar, flour, and other staples needed for the family."[17]

Many youth dropped out of school hoping to find employment to add to their family income but jobs for the young were practically nonexistent. New Dealers faced the very real possibility that the Depression generation would be one with many high school dropouts. The Texas public school aid program was organized by counties. A quota of jobs was assigned to each county by the state and NYA and school officials

5.2   The author's father and aunt both were part of the NYA. Their money allowed for electricity to be turned on in the family house as well as food for the family of six living in Clinton, Dewitt County. Author's collection.

within the county were then responsible for assigning those jobs. Public school officials were usually willing to work together in the program for they were anxious to help the youth stay in school. Jobs were assigned to each high school in the county and students applied directly to the principal of their school for NYA job after verifying the application. The young person had to be considered on relief status; this meant that his parents were either on the relief roles, employed by the Works Projects Administration (WPA) or the Public Works Administration (PWA), or in the Rural Rehabilitation program. Public school aid was labeled a godsend to needy students by many Texas educators, and assistance was extended to those over 16 years of age in the junior high or elementary grades to qualify for student aid.

Johnson issued an office memo in December 1935, to set the guidelines for sponsors in planning projects for their communities. Work sponsors were to ensure that the project accomplish two main goals. It was to provide "employment consistent with the needs of an occupational classification for youth available for the project" and to complete "work which will be useful to the community especially to young persons." The work also had to fall into one of four broad categories established by the national office: One category, "Projects for Youth Community Development and Recreational Leadership," included part-time employment for use as recreational leaders, assistance at parks, playgrounds, or community centers, the improvement of recreational facilities, and the development of programs to teach better health, safety, and sanitation practices. Another classification listed possible projects for rural youth such as disseminating information on improved farming techniques, establishing and providing recreational leadership for rural community or county centers, and "maintaining and enlarging rural library services." The third category called for initiating public service projects where local government agencies would employ NYA youth as assistance in valuable activities beyond their budgetary means. The fourth type listed was the research project. The sponsor could employ young people to conduct research for local histories or for the gathering of information to develop local campaigns to improve safety or health conditions. This memo specifically prohibited sponsors from developing major construction projects, a restriction which the national office later changed when it began to emphasize training. One of the most popular out of school work projects was the construction of roadside parks.[18]

Johnson successfully approached Gilchrist, the state Highway engineer, about the Texas Highway Department cosponsoring a program to build parks along the highways across the state. At these worksites NYA workers cleared the land, built rock benches and tables and constructed barbecue pits. The highway department provided the material and supervisors for the work while the NYA paid the youth workers' salaries. In June 1936, NYA employed approximately 3600 youths on this project and in the following months thousands more joined the ranks. The project was highly acclaimed by the public for aiding young people and for furnishing safer places on the narrow highway shoulders for weary travelers to rest.[19]

The NYA, however, fell short in employing young women, who in 1935 made up 53.9% of the youth on relief in Texas adding further to their desperation. Ninety-percent of them were unskilled. The NYA, therefore established sewing rooms around the state to employ young women in repairing second-hand garments and making new clothes to distribute in their communities. Few local government agencies were willing to sponsor the sewing room, so the NYA had to provide most of the supervision and materials. Some communities did furnish space and utilities for the projects. In the early months of operation many sewing rooms did not even supply sewing machines; work was done by hand.

5.3   At sixteen, Lem Reese Scoggin left his rural home in Clinton, Dewitt County, to work on the highways as a NYA employee. His money went to putting food on the table to feed his widowed father, grandmother, and his aunt and uncle and cousin. Author's collection.

Another highly innovative aspect of the state NYA was the resident training program designed for unemployed, out of school youths. Many of these young people were unskilled, and the NYA introduced a program to give them training and temporary employment at the same time. Resident training centers were established on college campuses and in communities throughout the state where resources and personnel were available to teach youth a skill or trade. In return for their instruction, the NYA residents worked either at their newly acquired skill or at unskilled labor in construction work. Those who participated in the resident training programs came from all areas of the state and lived at the center for two to four months. The resident training programs were widespread and diversified. They filled a special need for Texas youths and provided an example of the positive value of vocational education. These camps were plagued by the same problems as such centers in other states. The primary difficulty was that the girls' camps existed entirely for the benefit of the residents and offered nothing to the community. While attending an eight-week session of a NYA camp a young woman was taught "home management and elementary academic subjects."[20]

5.4   NYA girls, left to right, Ila Stevens, Lillie Stevens, Verna Stevens, Gladys Fudge, Effie Stevens at NYA Camp in Victoria County, Texas. Author's collection.

The girls' camp program was, perhaps, the least successful of those initiated by the NYA, but the positive benefit it had on the lives of those who participated should not be ignored. For "girls broken either spiritually or physically by the Depression years" the camps served "to restore their confidence, to teach them how to approach persons from whom they want employment . . . and how to occupy their time when there is no job to be had and no money with which to attend school."[21]

These resident training programs developed a wide range of live-in projects to improve the employment prospects for unemployed young women. In Cuero, Dewitt County, Texas, a two-story home served as live-in residence for NYA girls until 1941. The young women attended classes in nutrition, food service, meal planning, family health and disease prevention, proper behavior, home economics and elementary academics. Many of these girls also received their high school degrees (GED).[22]

5.5 NYA notebook. Author's collection.

The NYA intended for resident projects to reach rural youth and centers initially focused on agricultural activities. Boys raised crops for local welfare agencies, worked on the soil conservation projects, and took related training courses in crop diversification, care of farm equipment, and improved farming techniques. Young women attended classes in sewing, marketing, and canning at project sites. Their productive work might include sewing clothes for distribution by local relief agencies. Because of the success of the agricultural resident centers, the NYA began to approve projects that offered youth work experience and training in construction work, metalworking or automotive repair. In fact, resident projects could engage in any kind of activity as long as the work was beneficial to the community and provided enrollees with experience and training that would improve their chances for obtaining a job within their rural locality. NYA resident center experiences were also valuable because they offered more to young people than wages and work experience. Certainly, the approximately $22 per month which youth earned was a significant benefit. After sending home most their pay, the enrollees still had six dollars for personal use. For many the lodging and food offered them better physical and nutritional conditions than they had known before. In addition, the self-government training and experience encouraged at each project taught youthful workers to be responsible citizens. Years later, former participants who lived and trained at resident centers remembered another important but intangible benefit of their experience. Many of the NYA youths had lived only on family farms. In this isolated setting, their only close contacts were with relatives, sharing chores and living spaces. The centers helped them overcome their shyness and learn to compromise with others. Ruth Luder-Stevens an NYA youth used her opportunity to learn to deal with people beyond her family, a valuable step for her and later her family.[23]

The statistics which the state youth program was able to report were impressive. As of March, 1936, 11,030 high school students and 5,905 college students held part-time NYA jobs, 12,011 on work projects, and 631 as students in fifteen freshman college centers.[24] By November, 1936, the youth director in Texas was able to tell the Texas Press Association, "In short, it has touched the lives of over 30,000 youngsters who have been fighting for a toe-hold after the Depression; yet, it didn't give them one red cent they didn't work for and earn themselves."[25]

The impact of the National Youth Administration in Texas did not end with the abolishment of the program. Rather, it continued in the lives of those who administered the program and of those who worked in its various projects and for this author the NYA played a momentous role in my family's life and my own.

Notes and Acknowledgments

[1] Franklin Roosevelt, "Statement on the National Youth Administration.". June 26,1935. Online by Gerhard Peters and John T Woolley. *The American Presidency Project.* http://www.presidency.ucsb.edu/ws//pid=15091.

[2] Garth Akridge, Regional Director, "Brief Reports by Mr. Akridge on the States in His Region," Reports received from Field Representatives and Regional Directors,1935-1938 file, box 10, U.S. National Youth Administration Government Records, 1935-1938 (Lyndon Baines Johnson Library, Austin, Texas) [hereafter cited as NYA Papers].

[3] Wector, Dixon, *The Age of the Great Depression* (New York: MacMillan Co,.1948) p.187.

[4] Rosenman, *Papers of Roosevelt*, Vol 4, p. 286, states $109,170,612.00 was allocated to the NYA by June 3, 1937. Vol. 7, p. 227 states that on April 14, 1938, Roosevelt asked Congress for an additional $75,000.00 for the NYA for the fiscal year ending June 30, 1939.

[5] Ibid Papers of Roosevelt, Vol. 5, p. 230.

[6] Leuchtenberg, William, *Franklin D. Roosevelt and the NewDeal:1932-1940* (New York: Harper and Row, 1963.) p.129.

[7] Editorial, *Lubbock Morning Avalanche*, July 7, 1936 p. 3.

[8] Wector, p.188.

[9] Rosenman, *Papers of Roosevelt*, Vol. 8, p. 290.

[10] Telegram, Lyndon Johnson to Jacob Baker, August 30, 1935, *NYA Papers*, Johnson Library, Austin, Texas.

[11] *San Antonio Express*, March 30, 1935; *San Antonio Light* March 29, 31, 1935

[12] Federal Security Agency, Final Report to the NYA, 39-41; P. Johnson and Harvey, The National Youth Administration, 49;" The National Youth Administration of Texas," 2; Thelma McKelvey to Palmer O Johnson, memo, July 13, 1937, p.17, Miscellaneous Alphabetic Name Correspondence, 1935 1941 file, box 10, NYA Papers.

[13] P. Johnson and Harvey, *The National Youth Administration*, 27, 93-94; Federal Security Agency, Final Report of the NYA, 48;" The National Youth Administration of Texas," NYA Papers.

[14] Federal Security Agency, Final Report of the NYA, 51, 52 [quotation], 53, 246; Johnson to All Superintendents of Schools, memo Oct. 23, 1935, Administrative Reports: Nov.-Dec., 1935 file, box 5, NYA Papers.

[15] P. Johnson and Harvey, The National Youth Administration, 27, 93-94; Federal Security Agency, Final Report of the NYA, 48;" The National Youth Administration of Texas," NYA Papers.

[16] Federal Security Agency, Final Report of the NYA, 51, 52 [quotation],

53, 246; Johnson to All Superintendents of Schools, memo Oct. 23, 1935, Administrative Reports: Nov-Dec., 1935 file, box 5, NYA Papers.

[17] "Final Report, National Youth Administration, for the State of Texas" [95, 97]; Federal Security Agency, Final Report of the NYA, 56-58; Marian L Enke, Doris Echols Questionnaire to Carol Weisenberger, July 1990; Sam Gilstrap to J.C. Kellam, Dec. 7, 1938, Administrative Budget and Personnel: July-Dec., 1938 file, box 2, NYA Papers.

[18] Procedure for Development and operation of National Youth Administration Work Projects," Administrative Reports: Jan-Feb., 1936 file, box 5, NYA Papers.

[19] Administrative Reports: Oct-Dec., 1937 file, box 6, NYA Papers; J. Rex Ritter, "Organized Youth Builds Roadside Parks," Roads and Streets, Sept. 1937, pp.41-44, attached to "Texas Monthly Narrative Report for October 1937.

[20] *Dallas Morning News*, September 11, 1935, Sect. II, p.1.

[21] Cox, *Fort Worth Star-Telegram*, September 27, 1935, p.4.

[22] Oral history from Jewel Moore daughter of Ruth Luder Stevens, June 2017.

[23] Moore, oral history 2017.

[24] Texas NYA *Monthly Report*, April 1936, NYA Papers.

[25] Lyndon Johnson, "Government Making It Possible for Young Men and Women to Attend College," *Texas Press Messenger*, XI (September 1936), p. 4.

Part Two:
The New Deal and Texas Communities

I Too Sing "Texas, Our Texas": Black Texans and New Deal Community Service Projects

Ronald E. Goodwin

In 1926, Langston Hughes wrote "I, Too" giving a voice to the perilous plight facing African Americans living with the daily horrors of Jim Crow racism and the twin sisters of violence and segregation. In the second line Hughes states that he is the "darker brother" who is forced to "eat in the kitchen" when "company comes." It is a stark reminder that white America would never let its black citizens forget their supposed "place" in this society, a place where blacks were ever-present but strategically kept absent from public view.

However, there was also a ray of hope in Hughes' poem. He triumphantly states that out of the darkness he would rise "tomorrow" and eat at the "table." He concludes by stating: "Besides, they'll see how beautiful I am and be ashamed – I, too, am American." The end result was a poem that conveyed the contradictory nature facing Africans living in America: trying to maintain a culture that was summarily stripped away during centuries of slavery while they contributed greatly to the economic success of a society that barely acknowledges their humanity.[1]

Texas is a southern state. As such, vestiges of slavery and Jim Crow were manifested in tangible systems of racism that were very present in the 1930s. The eventual development of Franklin Roosevelt's New Deal, and particularly the Works Progress Administration (WPA), did not erase Jim Crow or those racist systems. But the WPA did provide jobs and hope that the government "by the people, for the people," would not turn away from those suffering under the weight of the Depression. For black Texans this was particularly hopeful. Just as Hughes argued that he too was an "American," blacks born and living in Texas considered themselves "Texans," which meant the state song, Texas, Our Texas, belonged to them as much as to any other.

Therefore, what follows is a brief examination of select New Deal/WPA operations and community service projects and their positive impacts on black Texans. Such projects literally changed lives throughout the state. Texans welcomed, though some hesitatingly, government involvement in the economy. More specifically, the black community welcomed projects involving music, recreation facilities, nursery schools,

Adult Education and food for the poor and disadvantaged not only for their economic benefits, but for the belief that the government would now insure a minimum standard of living.

Texas's frontier spirit of *rugged individualism* was still evident among the state's white elite after October 1929, but the economic crises wreaked havoc throughout the state.[2] Blacks were especially vulnerable to any economic, social and political "hiccup." For example, black unemployment increased from 4.8 percent in 1930 to 8.8 percent in 1933, while white unemployment only rose from 4.2 percent to 5.4 percent in the same period. New technological advancements, coupled with the reduction in cotton production, forced over 500,000 out of rural areas where some owned their own land, but a majority worked as tenet farmers. By 1937, blacks constituted 25 percent of the state's unemployed, while comprising only 14 percent of the total population.[3]

In Texas, as in other states throughout the country, private organizations initially provided economic relief to the hungry and homeless after 1929. In Houston, for example, the First Presbyterian Church provided meals to over 75, 000 individuals during the winter of 1930.[4] However, such private entities were not above Texas' racist norms of the day. Records indicate some private entities refused to distribute food or clothes to needy blacks and Hispanics because they felt there were not enough supplies to take care of the city's white families.[5] Another example of Texas' Depression-era racism occurred when Governor James Allred requested additional funds to increase the number of Civilian Conservation Corp (CCC) camps. Unfortunately, many Texans vocally expressed rabid opposition to any new CCC facilities that might possibly become predominately "Negro" camps, even though the existing CCC facilities were already racially segregated.[6]

Therefore, it was not surprising that blacks and Hispanics experienced the initial hardships of the Depression to a much greater degree than most whites. White families were not exempt from the despair of homelessness and poverty, but the state unemployment rate for blacks, was twice that of their white contemporaries.[7] Like the black community, Texas' Hispanic community did not escape hardships during the 1930s, but there was no significant change in their economic standing from the post-Reconstruction era when they struggled for political and social recognition and economic survival in Texas' changing economy.[8]

Once established in 1935, the WPA became a particularly transformative entity in Texas. The Operations Division sponsored construction-related projects providing jobs for thousands of blue-collar workers (both white and minority). For example, in 1935, during its first year of existence in Bexar County, the Operations Division sponsored fifty-four construction projects, the majority of which directly benefited the city of San Antonio, pumping over one million dollars into the city's economy through employee wages.[9]

These types of construction projects were typical throughout Texas. While some were small, they nonetheless filled a definite community need, especially in poor, minority-dominated communities, whose infrastructures and public facilities would have deteriorated further had it not been for the WPA. Thanks to WPA funds, blacks in the town of McKinney built a 30' by 35' building to be used as a school for 225 of its children.[10] In another instance, Dallas's black Oak Cliff community remodeled its segregated playground for use as a community center.

While the operations division focused on manual work, the state's community services projects (classified into three broad categories: Welfare, Community Services, and Research and Records) provided jobs and services throughout the state.[11] Welfare programs, especially those providing food, were particularly impactful as homelessness and unemployment decimated black and brown communities. Existing records indicate that many of those receiving assistance often wrote letters of gratitude to District officials. Lula Estelle and Lela Buggs, both of Marshall, Texas, said their families would have died of starvation had it not been for the surplus commodity project. Helen Riggins said, "Lord have mercy. Do I get all this many groceries? I do not ever remember having all this many groceries in my kitchen before. This is shore something for us old niggers to be proud of. I shore do thank you."[12] Likewise, Isaac Harper stated, "I just don't know what I would do if I did not get these groceries down here. I can tell you right now I appreciate what you all does for me."[13] Emma Moore of Waskom said, "I shore am glad to get these things. I likes it all. I'm not hard to please for I can't work anymore. I have to depend on the good white people, I thank you."[14] Finally, the District 16 commodities project provided meals for 2,285 school children and 3,920 indigent families mostly in minority communities.[15]

The sewing project in Gilmer, Texas, produced clothing for the State Colored Orphanage. In her letter to Virginia Chapman, Dorothy Wentland reported that the women of the project "have taken an interest in making the garments for these little Negro children."[16] She concluded her letter by commenting that not only did black children benefit, but also poor children of all races received clothing that was considered "excellent quality."[17]

Providing quality care for infant children was a concern for working parents. As a result, the WPA established nursery programs in practically every community throughout the state. Although many of the nurseries were racially segregated, they were still welcomed in their communities by parents with little or no childcare options. In San Antonio, there were two units of Nursery Schools in operation: one for Mexican children (located at 709 S. Frio Street) and the other for black children (located at 522 N. Center Street). Each unit had an average enrollment of 40.[18]

However, because of the racist atmosphere in San Antonio in the 1930s those assigned to work in minority nursery programs were not provided the same opportunities for professional development as those nursery programs for white children. Workers at the white nursery school programs had the opportunity to attend training conferences where they learned WPA policies and received leadership training. Conversely, those assigned to the "colored" schools only received training in crafts and other job-related skills.[19]

Even though those assigned to minority nursery programs did not have the same opportunity to further their education within the WPA, local black social and religious groups gladly sponsored "Negro" nursery schools throughout the state. Although their sponsorship was financially low during the summer months, donations from groups like the Negro Baptist Minister's Association and the Negro Physicians Association provided needed monetary support for those minority nursery schools in San Antonio. Furthermore, the Negro Baptist Minister's Association in San Antonio led the community in the development of an advisory board for the Negro nursery school.[20]

The white Missionary Societies in Gainesville collected and sold used magazines and newspapers for the support and maintenance of that community's black nursery school. Additionally, the wife of the local school principal in Gainesville visited the black nursery school and commented that the project was an asset to the community, as well as to the "Negro race."[21]

The WPA also established a Negro nursery school in Fort Worth that was conveniently located across the street from the Negro public school. To address the health needs of the children, the city's "Negro health nurse" visited the nursery each week. Even though there were established segregated nursery schools throughout the state, records indicated that there was still need for more Negro nursery schools.

Throughout the state, black religious leaders were extremely vocal in petitioning the WPA for the establishment of nursery schools that were convenient to their communities. The Reverend Marvin Robinson, of the Polly Chapel Baptist Church in Texarkana, and Reverend Rector, Pastor of San Antonio's West End Baptist Church, wanted to establish Negro nursery schools in their local communities. In Houston, the Pastor of Fifth Ward's Pleasant Hill Baptist Church, Reverend L.H. Simpson, also wanted a nursery for the predominantly black Fifth Ward after more than 200 parents attended parent education classes.[22]

Recognizing the need for increased education and training as a means of increasing employment opportunities, the WPA aggressively established Adult Education centers in as many communities as they could find qualified teachers. Even where there were teachers, they often underwent two weeks of training and were then placed under the supervision of trained teachers. In District 7, for example, teachers trained at North Texas Teacher's College, while in District 1, the Adult Education project established cooperative relationships between the WPA and the Stephen F. Austin State Teacher's College, which allowed the Red Bayou School to establish classes in Bowie County. In the black segregated programs, the District established cooperative agreements between Prairie View A&M College and Gethsemane Negro School.

Segregation played a role in the training of 136 Adult Education workers in District 4. The District's white teachers received training three hours per day, five days per week. The training for blacks followed a similar schedule but there were differences. Data indicated, "except that a few hours weekly were assigned to be done in the Negro branch of the City library. This work is carefully supervised, as are the hours of study in the workshop."[23] The supervisors in District 4 seemingly supported segregated programs when they recommended assigning three black teachers to the Rockwall County project to work with the predominantly black programs there. Rockwall had a higher percentage of "illiterate Negroes than any other County in the state" and they felt that only black teachers might be successful there.[24]

In San Antonio, where the training was also segregated, teachers were divided into three groups: two for whites and one for blacks. Adult Education programs operated at 41 schools, churches, and other community centers in the Greater San Antonio area. Men and women received elementary school, vocational, and Americanization training. Many in these classes were foreign born while others were native Texans who never had the opportunity to acquire even a grammar school education. By the spring of 1940, eighty-seven teachers were employed in San Antonio and taught literacy, general education, and vocational classes to over 2,600 individuals. Between March and November 1940, just over 6,000 students received some form of instruction, in addition to conducting 32 parent education meetings with nearly 2,500 in total attendance.[25]

District 7 also conducted classes for foreign-born adults in addition to their literacy classes for blacks. General education classes specifically designed for Hispanic were held in Eastland, Ft. Worth, and Cisco, plus a library class in Fort Griffin for whites. In those Districts along the Texas-Mexico border, though, officials reported numerous problems with the Hispanic Adult Education programs because participants did not attend classes regularly. They commented that the need to work outweighed the need to learn English. In Overton, District 1, officials established four new Adult Education classes in November 1940. However, these Adult Education classes were segregated: two specified for white children, and the other two for black children.

Lastly, one of the black workers in District 10, James Valentine, resigned from the Adult Education program in San Antonio to become the Pastor of a church in Athens, Texas. In his letter of resignation, Valentine thanked the WPA and the Adult Education program for providing him employment that helped him keep his home and put his daughter through college (Prairie View). Finally, Valentine stated "greatest of all, it (working with the WPA) gave me a chance to pursue my course of study and further prepare myself for the position as Pastor of one of our leading churches. I leave with regret, but shall ever do all I can do to further Adult Education and lift up my people."[26]

Even though Franklin Roosevelt's New Deal introduced a new level of government programing, it did little to erase the pervasive racism that existed in Texas and the nation. African Americans were still victims of racial stereotyping that denied the basic rights of all Americans cherished under the Declaration of Independence and the Constitution. The words, "We hold these truths to be self-evident, that all men are created equal," sadly rang hallow for those victims of racial hatred.

In Texas, the WPA provided jobs and also some encouragement that the legacy of slavery would actually begin to fade in earnest. Unfortunately, it would be another thirty years before African Americans would have federal protection from Jim Crow. Just as Langston Hughes' poetic argument that he was an "American" challenged this country to reexamine what it meant to be a citizen in a society that routinely ostracized part of its own populace, black Texans used the New Deal to demonstrate a resolve to survive the challenges caused by economic ruin. Not only did black Texans survive but they entered the World War II era willing to defend a Constitution that had yet to fully recognize their citizenship.

Notes and Acknowledgments

[1] See WEB DuBois, *Souls of Black Folk*

[2] "Rugged individualism" was a 19th century ideology that emphasized self-reliance and served as the basis for the later idiom of "pulling oneself up by their own bootstraps." The belief in capitalism and the opportunity to excel by one's own talents served as the model for European immigrants arriving in the late 19th and early 20th centuries. Many were very successful through hard work and shrewd business acumen. However, by the 1930s, Franklin Roosevelt believed a laissez-faire government was insufficient to deal with the present economic crises. The development of what became the "welfare state" continues to be debated today.

[3] Alwyn Barr, *Black Texans: A History of Negroes in Texas, 1528-1971* (Austin: Jenkins, 1973), 153-154. The number of black farm owners continued at about 20,000 in 1940; however, the number of black tenants had declined in the 1930s from 65,00 to 32,000.

[4] Marguerite Johnson, *Houston: The Unkown City 1836-1946* (College Station: Texas A&M University Press, 1991), 285. Even though racism existed in Houston, the author made sure the reader understood that benevolent organizations (churches) provided relief to all Houstonians regardless of "race and creed."

[5] Mike Kingston, *A Concise of History of Texas*, (Houston: Gulf Publishing Company, 1991), 200.

[6] Lionel Patenaude, *Texans, Politics, and the New Deal*, (New York: Garland, 1983), 107. In his article, "The Civilian Conservation Corps and the Negro," John Salmond found racism in the management of CCC camps was not restricted to Texas. Throughout the South blacks were systematically excluded from selection to CCC facilities, even though in many counties blacks constituted more than 50 percent of the population. Salmond also found the issue of racism in the selection process reached Franklin Roosevelt who failed to challenge the South's continued segregation and degradation of blacks. As with the issue of lynching, the President decided he would not risk his larger New Deal programs or his reputation by coming to the aid of blacks.

[7] Rupert Richardson, et al, *Texas: The Lone Star State*, (8th edition, New Jersey: Prentice Hall, 2001): 384.

[8] Two studies by Arnoldo De León illustrated the history and racism experienced by the Hispanic community in Texas. In *They Called Them Greasers* (Austin: University of Texas Press. 1983) De León focused on the discrimination faced by Mexicans during the period 1821-1900. He found that whites in Texas believed Mexicans were culturally inferior, Mexican women to be sexually promiscuous, and overall could not be trusted to be loyal American citizens. Like

blacks, Mexicans were routinely murdered and lynched. In *Ethnicity in the Sunbelt* (College Station: Texas A&M University Press, 2001) De León focused on the building of Mexican communities in Houston. In the 1930s, he found the Mexican community used the same strategy for survival as the black community, reliance on churches, cultural maintenance, and community self-reliance. Even though many Mexicans returned to Mexico during the Depression, De León found that those who stayed in Houston tried to end systematic racism through civil rights organizations: Latin American Club, League of United Latin American Citizens, and in the 1960s, La Raza. Likewise, in *The World of the Mexican Worker in Texas* (College Station: Texas A&M Press, 1993) Emilio Zamora found those Mexican communities along Texas' border regions, like those in the urban areas, also established social and labor organizations as a way of confronting the hardships of the Depression.

[9] *San Antonio Light*, October 20, 1940

[10] The building used for this segregated school was only 30 by 35 feet, and local blacks purchased the tin roof for only $10.00.

[11] Narrative Report, District 4, September 1940, Box 4F78.

[12] Narrative Report, District 1, November 1940, Box 4F78, Ibid.

[13] Ibid.

[14] Ibid.

[15] Narrative Report, District 16, March 1940, Box 4F82, WPA Records (CAH).

[16] Letter from Dorothy Wentland to Virginia Chapman, November 23, 1940, Narrative Report, District 1, December 1940, Box 4F78, Ibid.

[17] Ibid.

[18] Narrative Report, District 10, May 1940, Box 4F81, Ibid.

[19] Statewide Narrative Report, October 1940, 651.3142, WPA Central Files: Texas.

[20] Narrative Records, District 10, 1940, Box 4F81, WPA Records (CAH).

[21] Statewide Narrative Report, October 1940, 651.3142, WPA Central Files: Texas.

[22] Ibid; Narrative Report, District 1, November 1940, Box 4F78, WPA Records (CAH); Narrative Report, District 6, November 1940, Box 4F79, WPA Records (CAH); Narrative Report, District 10, November 1940, Box 4F81, WPA Records (CAH).

[23] Narrative Report, District 4, December 1940, Box 4F78, Ibid.

[24] Ibid.

[25] Narrative Report, District 10, May 1940, Box 4F81, Ibid.

[26] Letter of resignation from James Valentine, Narrative Report, District 10, November 1940, Box 4F81, Ibid.

The Construction of Huntsville State Park: Race and Recovery in Twentieth-Century East Texas

Carolyn A. Carroll and Jeffrey L. Littlejohn

Huntsville State Park has long been considered one of the great success stories from the New Deal era. The Civilian Conservation Corps (CCC) began construction on the park during Franklin D. Roosevelt's New Deal of the 1930s. At the time, government officials and local boosters promised that the park would provide visitors with a welcome respite from the economic conditions of the Great Depression. Design plans called for a large man-made lake for fishing, a beautiful stone lodge for relaxation, and scenic spots for bird watching. The park's initial construction phase came to an end, however, in November 1940, when a violent storm destroyed the park's spillway and lake. Despite local calls to repair the park, World War II and the Cold War delayed construction at the site for more than a decade. Finally, in March 1956, the park opened to the public with a new dam, spillway, and lake built by the Trinity Construction Company. Today, the park boasts a 2,100-acre wooded recreational area with 21 miles of hiking trails. Visitors can also enjoy fishing in Lake Raven, camping in one of the park's 160 campsites, and learning about the regional environment through interpretative ranger programs at Raven Lodge.

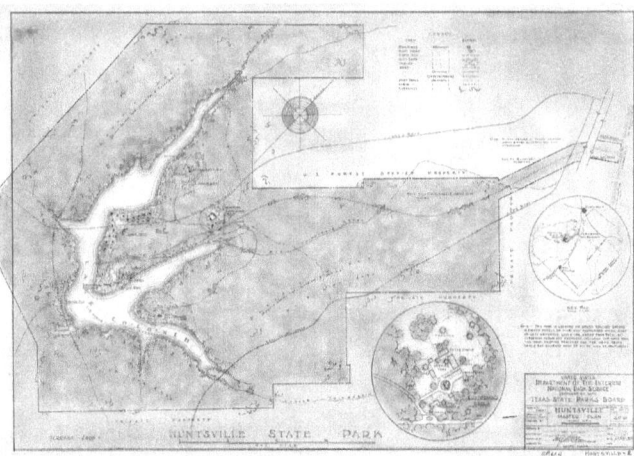

7.1   "Master Plan for Huntsville State Park." This Master Plan for Huntsville State Park was drafted in December 1937. It provided a clear overview of the park, including boundary lines, wildlife areas, and Lake Co-Lo-Neh. (Texas State Library and Archives).

Despite the bucolic setting at Huntsville State Park, the site has a complicated racial story that exposes some of the most painful ironies and contradictions in Texas history. Few campers today know that one of the park's initial construction crews, CCC Company 1823 Veteran Colored (VC), was an all-black unit of veterans from the Spanish American and First World wars. Although the men in this unit cut the hiking trails, reforested the landscape, and built the original spillway for the park, they were barred from visiting it and other state parks in Texas due to racial segregation. As attorneys for the National Association for the Advancement of Colored People (NAACP) fought against the obvious discrimination that African Americans endured in Texas, state park officials and local leaders in Huntsville and other cities around the state debated the best way to resolve the matter. In the short run, massive resistance against desegregation won the day. In fact, Texas governor Allan Shivers co-opted Huntsville State Park, and made it a rhetorical weapon in his campaign to stave off racial desegregation during the 1950s. By injecting "a state's right theme" into his dedication address at the park on May 18, 1956, Shivers called on white Texans to resist federal attempts to force the state to desegregate parks, schools, and other publicly-funded institutions. Shivers' tactics worked in the short-run, setting the stage for at least one racially-charged confrontation at Huntsville State Park in the 1960s. But Shivers and the segregationists lost in the end. The Civil Rights Act of 1964 required that public parks, like the one in Huntsville, be open to all people without regard to race or color.[1]

Huntsville State Park sits six miles southwest of Huntsville, Texas, within Walker County and the Sam Houston National Forest. The land at the site was originally used by logging interests during the timber boom of the late nineteenth and early twentieth centuries. Once populated with large stands of Loblolly pine, shortleaf pine, and various hardwoods, the park area experienced significant cutting by the Foster Lumber Company between 1880 and 1920. Luckily, however, the park area was never clear-cut, and by "the mid 1930s, the trees had come back, and the land was heavily wooded in second-growth pine, oak, and elm. Some virgin hardwood remained as well."[2]

With the onset of the Great Depression in the 1930s, Texans faced a terrible economic crisis. Timber, agriculture, industry, and other sectors all experienced significant declines. The value of Texas farms, for example, fell from $3.6 billion in 1930 to $2.6 billion in 1940. Livestock values fell by $100 million during the 1930s, and unemployment reached unprecedented levels, in some areas topping 25 percent. Private charities and beneficent organizations, like the Red Cross and Salvation Army, proved unable to address the varieties of problems caused by the Depression. And, as thousands of Texans lost their homes and livelihoods, people called for the state and federal governments to provide relief.[3]

President Herbert Hoover was reluctant to use the full power of the federal government to address the Great Depression, and in November 1932 he paid the price for his hesitancy. New York's Democratic Governor, Franklin Roosevelt, ran against Hoover, and, with help from Texans Jack Garner and Sam Rayburn, he won 89 percent of the popular vote in Texas. Promising the American people a bold New Deal, Roosevelt quickly went to work. In his famous first 100 days, he signed bills into law establishing the Federal Emergency Relief Administration (FERA), the Agricultural Adjustment Act (AAA), the National Industrial Recovery Act (NIRA), and the Tennessee Valley Authority (TVA).[4]

Roosevelt's most popular program from the first 100 days may have been the Civilian Conservation Corps, a job-creation effort that employed young men and veterans in forest and park conservation. On March 21, 1933, President Roosevelt sent a request to Congress to introduce a bill that would create the CCC and put 250,000 men to work on reforestation and soil conservation projects. Congress quickly passed the bill, and the President signed it into law on March 31, 1933. By May, enlistments in the CCC, often referred to as "Roosevelt's Tree Army," exceeded volunteer enlistments of military personnel during the Spanish American War. The Corps enlisted men 18 to 25 years of age, while older-aged veterans were supervised by active military officers under the purview of either the U.S. Department of Labor, the U.S. Department of Agriculture, or the National Park Service. The military divided the CCC into nine corps districts, and army officers predicted CCC enlistee enrollment would be more than "three time the entire strength of the regular army within the continental limits of the United States."[5]

By October 1934, the CCC had begun a variety of construction projects in Texas (called the 8th Corps District). Several prominent citizens in Huntsville, including William J. Lawson, the manager of the Huntsville and Walker County Chamber of Commerce, became aware of these projects and led a push for a local state park. It took roughly a year to get local backing but plans for a state park began in earnest at a planners' conference in December 1935. The following month, a public meeting was held to explain the components of an upcoming county-wide bond election that would support construction of the proposed state park. Advocates explained that approximately 3,000 acres of land north of Huntsville was being considered for the development of the "most beautiful site in the nation," which they promised would be open to the public seven days a week without an entrance fee. All the citizens of Walker County had to do was sign a petition calling for a bond election to purchase the land and deed the site to the state government for a park. Residents were told that the park would be "the greatest recreational, cultural, and economic proposition ever offered to Walker County," and the voters responded enthusiastically to the proposed site at Moffitt Springs. The bond election passed in February 1936 by an overwhelming majority. Local resident J. W. Oliphant, chairman of the citizen's committee for the park's creation, informed residents that the next step required the state to approve tentative plans prepared by local engineers and planners. Improvements to the site were expected to begin by early summer with the construction of the park directed by the Texas State Park Board. The Moffitt Springs site seemed to have every component needed, but, due to topographical concerns, state park officials soon suggested an alternative site six miles south of Huntsville. The site relocation set the park project back eighteen months.[6]

On February 2, 1937, representatives of the National Park Service, the Texas State Park Board, and Huntsville's Chamber of Commerce investigated a new tract of land southwest of Huntsville. Since 1911, this second site had been owned by the Foster Lumber Company, but no timber or development work had been done at the site for some time. Upon completion of the site investigation, officials agreed that the location met the requirements to be a state park, and they began working diligently to acquire the property. The following July, Letitia Foster Campbell, heir to the Foster Estate, deeded 2,042 acres to the state of Texas for the sum of $14,500.[7]

With the site now secured, officials began preparations for the arrival of conservation laborers. At the time, CCC Company 899 resided and worked in Huntsville.[8] Comprised solely of white men, the company's primary assignment was in soil conservation, reforestation, and fire prevention in Sam Houston National Forest. Local leaders in Huntsville, along with Congressman Nat Patton, who represented the district, wanted Company 899 assigned to the park project. In April 1937, William J. Lawson, executive secretary of the state park board of Texas and former manager of the Walker County Chamber of Commerce, reported his belief that Company 899 would be transferred to the park. Representative Patton seemed hopeful too. But, a month passed, then two, and still there was no decision. As local leaders became frustrated, the editor of the *Huntsville Item* pushed for action too. "[I]t is imperative," the paper said, "that some course be taken at once to get plans underway .... [T]his park will give employment to several hundred men."⁹

7.2 "With the Men at Huntsville, Texas." Enlistees in Civilian Conservation Corps Company 899 lived and worked in Huntsville, Texas, during the mid-1930s. (1936 Official Annual of the Civilian Conservation Corps, San Antonio District, 8th Corps Area).

Despite the appearance of delay, federal and state officials were acting behind the scenes. During the summer of 1937, the Interior Department ended Company 899's forest service program and sent its members to another location. This decision, in turn, had important implications for the Huntsville park project. With Company 899 out of the way, federal officials wanted to know if Huntsville would accept a different, all-black unit of the CCC to construct the new state park. In August, J.C. Roak, a liaison officer with the 8th Corps, wrote to Herbert Maier, the CCC's regional supervisor in Oklahoma City, to inquire about the matter. "It would be appreciated," Roak said, "if you would continue the necessary negotiations" and advise me when "it is satisfactory to the people [of Huntsville] to accept these colored companies."¹⁰

Negotiations over "colored companies" were necessary, as historian Kenneth E. Hendrickson Jr. has argued, because "the handling of the race question" was among "the least attractive aspects of the CCC operations in Texas."[11] Although the CCC did not begin life as a segregated organization, the group's national director, Robert Fechner, was a Southerner who gave into local calls to segregate and exclude African Americans from CCC service. In fact, Fechner had the support, in most cases, of President Roosevelt, who "generally avoided issues of race [and] ethnicity" because he "feared the cultural and political battles" such issues might bring to the Democratic Party.[12] As a result, Fechner acted as he saw fit. According to Hendrickson, he "ordered that all camps in the South be strictly segregated and that no African Americans be sent out of their home states." In addition, Fechner decided in 1935 to limit the number of African American corps members in each state. Texas received only 3,200 spots for blacks, although some estimates placed the unemployment rate for black men nationwide as high as 40 percent. Further complicating matters was the fact that African Americans served under the direction of an all-white officer corps and often experienced racial discrimination. Eventually, under President Roosevelt's orders, black military officers, instructors, and clergy took the place of white officials. Even with this change, however, racial tensions remained prevalent inside and outside the camps. Many communities did not want African American camps situated nearby. One CCC Company, for example, was forced to move from a work project in Sweetwater, Texas, because of complaints from local whites about African American men walking through town. That is why the Parks Department had to have assurances from the City of Huntsville that the citizenry would approve the presence of an all-black unit.[13]

When the race question was finally put to William J. Lawson, he wrote to H.G. Webster, the vice president of the Huntsville National Bank and a leading proponent of the park. Webster and his allies approved the idea, and Lawson visited Huntsville to get support from the City Council, Chamber of Commerce, and local citizens. The community quickly approved the idea and requests were made for CCC Company 1823 (VC).[14] This company had originated from an integrated veteran company of two hundred white and 12 black veterans from Fort Sill, Oklahoma, that had disbanded in 1935. Reformed as a colored veterans' unit, Company 1823 (VC) had previously worked on the construction of several state park sites, including Palmetto State Park near Gonzales. Huntsville park planners wanted Company 1823 (VC) immediately transferred to the local area, and Representative Patton sent a volley of letters and wires to Washington demanding as much. After persistent requests, not only from

Patton but from three other local citizens--A. F. Randolph, H. G. Webster, and William Lawson--federal officials announced that Company 1823 (VC) would arrive in Huntsville in October 1937. In response, the local paper stated: "The successful culmination of a dream of a few citizens is due to the patience and untiring work of these three men." Designated as State Park 61, the Huntsville site received 200 men ready to work on Monday, October 24, 1937. The dream now seemed to be close to realization. As the editor of the *Huntsville Item* said: "all outstanding psychiatrists admit the best way to combat crime and to cure social unrest, is to build recreational centers for the youths of the land." According to the editor and many Walker County residents, Huntsville State Park would be the finest recreational center found in the state of Texas.[15]

7.3   "Company 1823 at Kerrville, Texas, presents some of its personnel." This montage of images from Kerrville, Texas highlights the activities of Company 1823 (CV) on the eve of their move to Huntsville, Texas. (1936 Official Annual of the Civilian Conservation Corps, San Antonio District, 8th Corps Area).

Following the design criteria established by the National Park Service, officials estimated that Huntsville State Park would take 4 to 5 years to complete. With the arrival of Company 1823 (VC) in Huntsville, program officers began setting up housing and administration facilities. Yet, the camp was not simply a workplace. Corps leaders emphasized the important opportunities for personal growth and education that were being offered to enlistees at each site. In the 1936 CCC Camp Yearbook (San Antonio District), for example, camp personnel reported that Company 1823 (VC) had engaged with "educational subjects" that would increase "their intelligence and culture," thereby making them of "greater value to employers." The report also mentioned that enrollees took literacy classes to help them achieve job readiness by the end of their enlistment.[16]

When Company 1823 (VC) moved to Huntsville, however, enlistees found the educational and betterment programs to be wanting. According to a quarterly report submitted in January 1938, the Huntsville superintendent indicated that local education programs were not yet on track. In fact, it took several months for instructors from the Huntsville area to get organized, and when they did, official documents show that they pursued a discriminatory educational program. As the superintendent bluntly reported, "in view of the fact that this is a Colored Veterans Company it is essential that training be conducted in an entirely different manner to other companies." The superintendent's report to the Acting Regional Director of the National Park Service revealed the depth of racial discrimination in the federal and state system. Since the enrollees of Company 1823 (VC) were black veterans, "the educational programs were principally concerned with making those subjects available which would provide beneficial knowledge to the men to utilize upon returning to their home towns." Although this type of vocational programming was common in both white and black camps, officials in Huntsville implied that black enlistees had little desire to attend academic classes, favoring instead athletic and musical programs. These assessments were made by white officers and seem to have been directly contradicted by the men of Company 1823 (VC).

We know what the men of 1823 thought about education and self-betterment because they addressed the two issues in their camp newspaper. Throughout the CCC, newspapers were printed to capture life in the camps so that family members and the outside communities could get a sense of what was going on and the importance of the enlistees' work. Many of the newspapers were supervised by the education advisors. In the black camps, papers promoted black awareness by highlighting the accomplishments of African Americans. One camp had a section titled "Who's Who in Colored USA." The papers encouraged enrollees to improve themselves through education that "would produce a good work ethic, which in turn would promote their attention to personal conduct, health and appearance."[17]

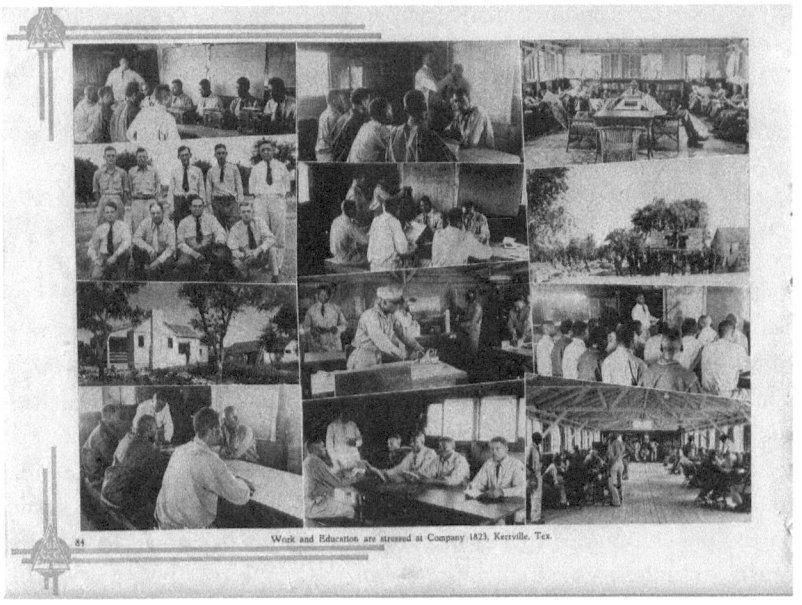

7.4 "Work and Education are stressed at Company 1823, Kerrville, Texas." This collection of images from Kerrville, Texas, showcases the educational activities that members of Company 1823 (CV) participated in before their move to Huntsville, Texas. (1936 Official Annual of the Civilian Conservation Corps, San Antonio District, 8th Corps Area).

The camp newspaper for Company 1823 (VC) rolled out its first edition in September 1937, while still assigned to the Ottine Camp in Gonzales County, Texas. This edition did not have a name, so the commanding officer started a five-dollar contest to come up with a suitable publication title. This prize money was quite enticing considering that the average enlistee received only thirty dollars per month, with the bulk of the earnings sent to family members. With many men entering the contest, the commander wanted the enlistees to understand that this newspaper was based on their opinions and not that of the Army or advisory personnel. The camp newspaper, eventually titled The Park Builder, opened with an editorial:

> We have passed through a period of universal upheavals. We have faced many financial losses, unemployment, hunger, and in many cases domestic tranquility has fled leaving us with unhappy homes. Even though

> we have endured many trials and hardships we yet have many reasons to be thankful! With this, our first issue, we the members of Company 1823, Veteran Colored, salute the world with a smile; as we are not about to die but with each educational, religious, and social effort made we are learning to BETTER LIVE!

This edition of the newspaper showed that enlistees actively participated in a variety of entertainment programs. From November 1935 to September 1937, for example, the company performed over sixty-three camp plays. The audience was comprised of both enlistees and nearby community members, both white and black. Camp records show that more than 10,000 local residents attended plays during this period.

The October 1937 edition of The Park Builder announced Company 1823's impending relocation to Huntsville. The various contributors to the paper praised their instructors for their work and expressed a sense of sadness and trepidation about the move to a new place. The fact that Huntsville housed the state penitentiary seemed to frighten some of the enlistees. One author, aware of the fear, assured his fellow enlistees: "don't worry as the pen was built for bad men, not veterans. Because veterans are all real men who stand for something other than immoral conduct. Don't worry boys, get ready and let's get going."[18]

After their October 1937 arrival in Huntsville, Company 1823 (VC) published its first camp newspaper in November. That month, the paper's editors and contributors gave thanks for the educational opportunities in the CCC. Indeed, one author noted that the company had left a community of "Friendly Neighbors and arrived at another friendly community," which would, he hoped, "support their educational ... [and] spiritual needs." This optimism proved to be justified, at least in the short run. In December, for example, local Huntsville women provided a program of musical numbers, and, during intermission, a local arts and crafts group displayed exhibits. Encouraged by local community support, approximately 246 people came to the program.

Yet, many of the enlistees in Company 1823 (VC) did not feel that camp officials or local residents supported their efforts. In February 1938, for example, The Park Builder addressed racism against African Americans through a poem titled "Trees" that appeared on the cover page. Written by the well-known American poet Abbie Farwell Brown, the poem began: "However, little I may be, At least I, too, can plant a tree. And some day it will grow so high That it can whisper to the sky."

The enlistees personalized this poem, which they saw as a metaphor for their individual growth. In a related poem on page one of the paper, an unnamed camp member wrote the following:

> We will start out to obtain such knowledge through the facilities found in the camp educational program. AT ONCE many of the members of the camp personnel will with derisive smiles and scornful remarks tell you, with extreme contempt and haughty disdain, that for a man such as YOU, AND AT YOUR AGE, to even attempt learning anything NOW is just a waste of your time: and the UNWORTHY effort of a FOOL.... Then during some CRISIS (sultry summer day), the people sheltered in the shades cast by the influence of a dream Realized will say: Oh, good and wise and great was he who did not let derision and scorn STOP him from PLANTING THIS BLESSED TREE.

This creative resistance sparked a response from CCC personnel. The same month that this poem appeared, a new educational program was implemented at the Huntsville camp to address the enlistees' concerns. Writers for the Park Builder encouraged enlistees to attend the new classes and said that doing so would make them a greater race and help them be more efficient providers for their families. Along with classes, the local African American community leaders came to the camp for observance of Negro History Week. Among the group was Dr. James Arthur Johnson, the first black dentist in Walker County, and K H. Malone, Sr. the agricultural extension agent for local African Americans. Both men addressed the business and educational outlook for blacks, along with on the job training.[19]

In February 1939, the Civilian Conservation Corps celebrated its sixth anniversary. Huntsville's enlistees designated Easter Sunday, April 9, and Tuesday, April 11, as celebration days. Despite the festive spirit, Easter's religious service and egg hunt were totally segregated. The program then continued by honoring the white Huntsville citizens involved in obtaining a state park for the area. The program included singing by the camp's glee club, and, for the enjoyment of many, it was broadcast over radio station KSAM in Huntsville. Later, the following Tuesday, the enlistees wrapped up the celebration with a barbecue.[20]

7.5 "The Park Builder." Civilian Conservation Corps Company 1823 (CV) named its newspaper The Park Builder. Only a handful of original copies of the paper still exist. This cover, from the April 1939 edition, highlights the sixth anniversary of the CCC. (Author's collection).

After the celebration, work continued, and, by the following August, the racial character of Company 1823 (VC) came up again. William Lawson wrote the Regional Director of the National Park Service and requested that 1823 be removed and replaced with an all-white junior company. He argued that this was necessary because the remainder of the projects in Huntsville required construction skills that were not ordinarily found in black veterans' camps. Park officials considered the request but finding a community that would accept the African American unit proved challenging. Officials tried the Austin area because of its liberal reputation but had little success. In a confidential memo to the acting regional director, a local inspector named John C. Diggs stated: "the City Administration would most likely be opposed to placing a Negro Company at the Park and would not even vote on the matter due to negative publicity." Diggs gave two reasons for resistance to an all-black company in Austin: "1. More work would be done by white enlistees and 2. Although Austin has a considerable percent of Negroes, there are no Negroes in the hill section west of the city and the native 'Mountaineers' of that area are strongly opposed to negroes." Shortly after this memo, due to a change in sentiment from Huntsville planners, they withdrew the request to transfer 1823.[21]

In 1939, enlistees continued work on the dam and started construction of the boat house, which would store recreational equipment for the newly built lake, named Co-Lo-Neh (the Cherokee's nickname for General Sam Houston). This lake, commonly known as Lake Raven, was designed to be the main attraction for Huntsville State Park. In March, park officials announced that Lake Raven was nearly complete and would be opened for recreational use the following June. From the start of the Huntsville park project to December 1940, numerous accomplishments were made by the CCC workers. Along with the boathouse, fishing and diving piers were constructed, a banquet lodge with a dance terrace was built, and road improvements, camp sites, land surveys, and wildlife studies were undertaken. With increased public awareness of the park's construction progress, thousands of visitors stopped to see the site and watchmen were hired to patrol the park at all times. The watchmen resided at the park with their families in separate quarters provided by the park service.[22]

The Huntsville park project continued as scheduled until a devastating flood event in November 1940. Between November 21 and November 24, the area around the park received approximately twelve inches of rain. Because of the vast amount of rainfall in a short time, the dam at Elkins Lake situated a few miles upstream from the park failed sending a torrent of water downstream. One of the watchmen at the park site heard the roaring water approach in the early hours of November 24, 1940. The force of the water along with continue rainfall caused a breach in the Lake Raven spillway, resulting in the complete drainage of water from the lake.[23]

On January 27, 1941, the Huntsville park superintendent and local engineers inspected the spillway failure at Lake Raven. After gathering information, the group submitted a formal report of its findings and an estimate of the costs that would be involved to rebuild the dam. The park project had already reached $700,000 in CCC funds, along with other federal and state expenditures. Getting additional funds proved most challenging. In the cost report for the repairs, the park inspector stated that the "entire HSP project was dependent upon the successful re-creation of Lake Raven." If this did not occur, he said, the funds paid out so far would be practically useless. Letters continued back and forth between officials indicating the uncertainty of obtaining funds for the repairs. To help ease the financial burden of rebuilding the lake, William Lawson, now Texas Secretary of State, contacted an official at the National Park Service in Washington, D.C., suggesting that the Work Progress Administration (WPA) could provide funds. The issue was not just budgetary, however. Conflict in Europe had begun as Germany invaded Poland on September 1, 1939, causing American leaders to shift their attention elsewhere. Then, on December 7, 1941, Japan attacked the United States Naval Base near Honolulu, Hawaii, drawing America into World War II and ending the Great Depression. During the war, many CCC workers enlisted in the military and funds for domestic projects dried up almost entirely. By April 1942, termination orders to CCC personnel were being activated and soon all projects came to an end, including the one at Huntsville State Park.

No additional work occurred at the park until 1953. At that time, the Huntsville and Walker County Chamber of Commerce gathered community support to fund the completion of the park. The principal source of money came from the park itself. The Texas Forest Service determined that enough timber could be harvested from the park to pay for the remaining construction costs. To retain the scenic value of the park's entrance, the mature trees along the road were exempt from harvest. A local contractor, Trinity Construction Company, was hired to build a new dam, which was completed in April 1956. Lake Raven quickly filled up. The road into the park was hard topped, and prisoners from the Texas Department of Criminal Justice spruced up the areas around the lake in time for the local dedication ceremony on May 18, 1956.

7.6   "Huntsville State Park Dedication Ceremony, May 18, 1956." Huntsville State Park opened with pomp and circumstance on May 18, 1956. Governor Allan Shivers gave a keynote address highlight the role that local citizens played in rebuilding the park after a devasting flood in 1940. (Springfield Collection, Huntsville Arts Commission).

At that time, Governor Allan Shivers used the park's opening to celebrate local know-how, while he ridiculed the federal government and its efforts to interfere in the affairs of the state. By inserting "a state's right theme" into his dedication address, Shivers hoped to encourage white Texans to resist federal attempts to desegregate parks, schools, and other publicly-funded institutions in the aftermath of the U.S. Supreme Court's decision in Brown v. Board of Education (1954). White Texans in Huntsville and the surrounding area did as Shivers hoped they would, protesting federal interference in local matters. In fact, a few years after Shivers' address, Sam Houston State Teachers College professor Rupert Koeninger took his sociology students and a distinguished African American guest, Reverend William "Bill" Lawson of Wheeler Baptist Church in Houston, to the park for lunch. To Koeninger's disgust, however, the park ranger refused to allow Reverend Lawson into the park and asked the group to leave immediately.[24] All of this, despite the fact that Company 1823 (VC) had devoted more than two years to the development of the park in the 1930s. In the end, it fell to one of Franklin Roosevelt's most vigorous and outspoken supporters, the famous Texan Lyndon

Baines Johnson, to right the situation, which he did when he signed the Civil Rights Act of 1964, forbidding racial segregation in public facilities across the United States.[25]

7.6 "Huntsville State Park Postcard." After 1964, Huntsville State Park opened to all people on an equal basis. Each year, thousands of visitors enjoy the hiking, swimming, and scenic beauty offered by the New Deal project.

Endnotes

[1] Huntsville State Park Dedication Program, "Huntsville State Park" vertical file, John Thomason Special Collections Room, Newton Gresham Library, Sam Houston State University; *Huntsville Item*, May 17, 1956.

[2] *A History of Huntsville State Park Walker County, Texas* (Waco, Texas: Baylor University Institute for Oral History, 1997), 13-14.

[3] *Randolph Campbell, Gone to Texas: A History of the Lone Star State* (New York: Oxford University Press, 2003), 378.

[4] Ibid.

[5] Vertical Files, Walker County Folder, Genealogy Room, Montgomery County Public Library, Conroe, Texas. Texas Research Institute for Environmental Studies in Conjunction with the Walker County Historical Commission, (Huntsville, Texas: Sam Houston Press, 1998) 3, hereafter cited as Walker County Folder. Associated Press, "Roosevelt Asks Power to Put 250,000 Men to Work on Reforestation," The *Houston Chronicle*, March 21, 1933. Robert E. Connor, "350 Men Are Expected To Get Work in Construction At CCC Camps In Texas," The *Houston Chronicle*, October 15, 1933, 14. "Associated Press, Enrollment for Tree Army To Be Completed Soon," The *Houston Chronicle*, May 26, 1933, 10. Official Annual, 1936 Civilian Conservation Corps, Lufkin District 8th Corps Area, John Thomason Special Collections Room, Newton Gresham Library, Sam Houston State University.

[6] "Bond Issue to be Explained at Meeting Sat," *Huntsville Item*, January 9, 1936. "Walker County Votes Bond Issue for Establishment of 3000 Acre Park," The *Houston Chronicle*, February 10, 1936. Vertical Files; "A Park for Walker County," park study in HSP Folder.

[7] A History of Huntsville State Park Walker County, Texas (Waco, Texas: Baylor University Institute for Oral History, 1997), 33.

[8] Company 899 had been formed in Oklahoma in June 1933 and arrived in Huntsville, Texas, in October 1935.

[9] "Park Development for Forest Studied," *Huntsville Item*, February 4, 1937, 7; A History of Huntsville State Park Walker County, Texas (Waco, Texas: Baylor University Institute for Oral History); "State Park," *Huntsville Item*, July 22, 1937.

[10] Correspondence between J. C. Roak, Liason Officer, CCC and Herbert Maier, Regional Officer, National Park Service (NPS), August 31, 1937 in CCC Park Huntsville, Group 79, Box 120, National Archives at Denver, Colorado, hereafter cited as CCC Park.

[11] Kenneth E. Hendrickson, Jr., "Replenishing the Soil and the Soul of Texas: The Civilian Conservation Corps: The Lone Star State as an Example of State-Federal Work Relief During the Great Depression," *Historian*, (Summer 2003) 801-816.

[12] Alan Brinkley, *The End of Reform: New Deal Liberalism in Recession and War* (New York: Vintage Books, 1995), 9

[13] Hendrickson, "Replenishing the Soil and the Soul of Texas," 801-816. Alfred Emile Cornebise, *The CCC Chronicles: Camp Newspapers of the Civilian Conservation Corps, 1933-1942* (Chapel Hill, North Carolina: McFarland & Company, Inc, 2004) 158-175. Cynthia Brandimarte, *Texas State Parks and the CCC: The Legacy of the Civilian Conservation Corps* (College Station, Texas: Texas A&M University Press, 2013), 52. The nearest CCC camp for African Americans from Walker County was in Coldspring, Texas, some thirty miles southeast of Huntsville.

[14] Walker County Folder, Texas Research Institute for Environmental Studies, 3; Official Annual, 1936 Civilian Conservation Corps, Lufkin District 8th Corps Area, Thomason Room, Sam Houston State University, Huntsville, Texas.

[15] Correspondence between J. C. Roak, Liason Officer, CCC and Herbert Maier, Regional Officer, National Park Service (NPS), August 31, 1937 in CCC Park Huntsville, Group 79, Box 120, National Archives at Denver, Colorado, hereafter cited as CCC Park. "Congressman Patton Busy," *Huntsville Item*, September 23, 1937, 6. "CCC Camp Ordered Here," *Huntsville Item*, September 6, 1937. Correspondence between Wm J. Lawson, executive secretary, NPS to Regional Director, Region III, NPS, August 27, 1937, in Box 117, CCC Park. "Recreational Centers," *Huntsville Item*, November 18, 1937, 6. Correspondence between Wm. J. Lawson and Regional Director, NPS, September 9, 1937, in Box 120, CCC Park.

[16] Official Annual, 1936 Civilian Conservation Corps, San Antonio District 8th Corps Area, provided by Texas Parks and Wildlife Department, Historic Sites and Structures Division, Austin, Texas. Hereafter cited TPWD.

[17] *The Park Builder*, Vol 1 No 1, September 1937 provided by TPWD. Official Annual, 1936 Civilian Conservation Corps, San Antonio District 8th Corps Area, provided by TPWD. Correspondence between M J. Nash, superintendent to Action Regional Director, NPS, January 31, 1938, in Box 122, CCC Park. Cornebise, 158-175. Park CCC Educational Training Plan, in Box 122, CCC Park.

[18] *The Park Builder*, Vol 1 No 2, October 1937 provided by TPWD.

[19] According to scholar Alfred Emile Cornebise, CCC camp newspapers stressed spiritual betterment through religious means in all black enlistee camps. Cornebise stated that in many ways the white and black camp papers were very similar in structure but stood out with content. Cornebise, 15-175. *The Park Builder*, Vol 1 No 5, February 1938, provided by TPWD. Naomi W. Lede, Ed., *Pathfinders: A History of the Pioneering Efforts of African Americans Huntsville, Walker County, Texas* (Virginia Beach: Donning Co., 2004).

[20] *The Park Builder*, Vol 3 No 4, April 1939 provided by TPWD. "Program Lined Up of Local CCC Camp For Celebration," *Huntsville Item*, March 24, 1938, 3. "Huntsville CCC will celebrate 6th Anniversary," The *Houston Chronicle*, 9

[21] Correspondences between Wm. J. Lawson to Hillory A. Tolson, Regional Director, NPS, August 16, 1939; Herbert Maier to Wm. J. Lawson, August 23, 1939; John C. Diggs, Inspector to Acting Regional Director, NPS November 14, 1939; Frank E. Quinn, executive secretary to Herbert Meier, November 14, 1939.

[22] Attendance figures: from June 1938 to August 1938, records indicated that 1,898 visitors stopped by the site. With such interest, park officials were encouraged and continued gathering data. Correspondence between L. C. Fuller, State Supervisor Recreation Study to Acting Regional Director, NPS, August 22, 1938.

[23] Huntsville State Park Project completion report January 3, 1941 in Box 117, CCC Park. "Lake at New State Park is Nearly Ready." *Houston Chronicle*, March 12, 1939, 9. Huntsville State Park Spillway Failure Report, January 1941, in Box 121, CCC Park. Memo to CCC district San Antonio from Dudley B. Jones, CCC Commander HSP, March 21, 1940, in Box 117, CCC Park.

[24] Frieda Koeninger, interviewed by Carolyn A. Carroll, Huntsville, Texas, September 2011.

[25] Memo on park costs and cost of dam repair from Inspector Rias to Director of Region III, NPS, May 12, 1941, in box 121, CCC Park. Correspondences between Conrad Wirth and Wm J. Lawson, September 2, 1941 & December 3, 1941, in Box 121, CCC Camp. Telegram NPS Director Washington Re: CCC personnel termination, April 8, 1942, in Box 120, CCC Park. BOH, p. 31-33. Walker County Folder, Texas Research Institute for Environmental Studies.

"Nature Has Provided a Park in the Rough": Caddo Lake and the CCC

Milton S. Jordan

In the summer of 1934 citizens of Harrison County, Texas, organized a "two-way celebration – July Fourth and the semi-opening of Caddo Lake State Park."[1] The celebration began at 9 a.m. on the courthouse square in downtown Marshall, the county seat, with band music, group singing and, of course, patriotic political oratory. The motorcade that followed headed northeast out of Marshall to the park site where Big Cypress Bayou empties into Caddo Lake. At this barely begun state park celebrants enjoyed a "great family style picnic," pot-luck dishes and food offered for sale by on site vendors. More music followed, with a boat parade on the bayou and shooting matches. Singing and dancing continued into the evening with addresses by state and area politicians.[2] The crowds, later estimated near a thousand (perhaps a politician's estimate) were celebrating the dedication of what was then called SP 1T, where the Civilian Conservation Corps, the CCC, first began constructing a state park in Texas.

Conservation-minded Texans had been pushing for a system of parks in the state for years, but legislation to set up the system seldom got beyond committee hearings. In 1927, though, Margie Elizabeth Neal, the first woman elected to the Texas Senate, introduced the bill that officially established the State Parks Board.[3] Neal, an East Texan from Panola County, was a newspaper publisher and an outspoken advocate for land conservation and later for Franklin D. Roosevelt's New Deal programs. Neal later served in Roosevelt's New Deal administration.[4] Sporadic state support for the parks board and often bitter interagency competition prevented much noticeable progress in establishing actual parks in Texas at the time, and the Great Depression eroded the state's already limited financial support.[5]

When Herbert Hoover was president Texas had only eight hundred acres of state park land. That situation was soon to change. Thanks to the New Deal, particularly the Civilian Conservation Corps, the acreage soared by 1942 to sixty thousand acres. State parks were located in every corner of Texas, from a clear, spring fed swimming pool at Balmorhea to a Cypress filled (not so clear) fishing hole at Caddo Lake.[6] Over 50,000 young men worked in the Civilian Conservation Corps on these Texas parks. Women were never included in the CCC.[7]

Roosevelt had pushed the bill establishing the Emergency Conservation Work program, of which the CCC was the primary component, through Congress a few weeks after his inauguration and on June 5, 1933, barely two months after the program was authorized one of the first CCC project superintendents, Walter K. Boggs, arrived at Caddo Lake in the northeast corner of Texas. With government and civic leaders of Marion and Harrison Counties Boggs toured the area and was impressed. In Caddo Lake, he said, "Nature has created a park in the rough." In a few days the first CCC camp officially assigned to Texas was designated for the lake. It was one of the first state park CCC camps in the country.[8] Co. 889 arrived on June 17 to begin SP1-T. Later, with a different company of corpsmen Caddo Lake was designated SP27-T and finally SP40-T.[9] Company 889 began site preparation work clearing brush and building roads and bridges but spent only a few months at the Caddo Lake site. A particularly rainy winter and early spring in 1934 left a worse than usual infestation of mosquitos at the site. Malaria became a serious problem with much sickness and one fatality.[10] The U.S. Army, which was responsible for operating all CCC camps nationwide, recommended abandoning the project entirely. But, in April Herbert Maier, National Park Supervisor for the region, telegraphed the acting superintendent at Caddo: "Do not give up on Caddo Lake unless you absolutely have to. Army may be bluffing as at Chisos." The ins and outs of CCC work at Chisos Basin in the Big Bend region are another story that is certainly worth some attention. Later that spring Co. 889 was transferred away from the swampy bogs along Big Cypress Bayou to a camp near Marble Falls to work on sites along the Colorado.[11] This may explain the line on that summer's Caddo Lake Picnic program, "Semi-Opening of Caddo Lake State Park system." By mid-summer, 1934, Emergency Conservation Work on the park site had stopped and no one was sure when or if it might begin again. Still, Northeast Texas community leaders hoped Caddo Lake State Park would be completed and serve as the anchor for a series of parks in Harrison and surrounding counties.[12]

Superintendent Maier must have been right on the Army's bluff. He gained political support from two prominent East Texans, long serving U.S. Senator and Chair of the Senate Armed Services Committee, John Morris Shepherd, from Morris County, and Cass County native J.W. Wright Patman, newly elected member of Congress from House District 1.[13] So, after a summer of inactivity, a new CCC company was assigned to work at Caddo Lake. The campsite for the new company was moved up Big Cypress Bayou a mile or so from the water-logged camp of Co. 889. George Mason, Senior Inspector for Emergency Conservation Work in the area, wrote Superintendent Maier on August 9, ". . . it will be necessary to move the camp from the old tent campsite [and] to provide a new well."[14] The new camp was occupied by CCC Co. 857 in October, 1934.[15]

Many of this group of corpsmen had spent the previous year building the dam and preparing the site for Grayson County Lake quite near Denison. As that project neared completion, the company prepared for its move to the much different Caddo Lake site. Harold Buckles, editor of the camp newsletter, *The 857 Log*, at both sites, described the move in his first Caddo Lake issue. "The outfit moved . . . to Caddo Lake State Park Oct. 15, to find itself in a spanking new camp."[16] The not yet completed camp was nice enough, but isolation proved a problem, according to Buckles. "Members of the company find it more difficult here to obtain transportation to nearby towns. While but a mile from Karnack, there is little there to amuse even CCCers."[17]

Other than the isolation, Buckles seems to have found the new location at the lake in deep woods to be "one of the great beauty spots of Texas." He did not write of health issues nor of the sometimes-boggy conditions. That was not the case for at least one of his contributors. A Local Experienced Man who had transferred from Grayson County, with Company 857, Joe Westbrook, Esq. as he signed himself, offered his views in this "Ode to A Swamp."

> It's the mud------gray mud
> The sloshy, grimy, slimy & sticky gray mud----gray mud.
> I go tramping, stamping, my muscles are cramping
> From mud----gray mud.
> I am crawling, falling and awkwardly sprawling
> In mud----gray mud.
> My temples are pounding, pounding and pounding
> From mud----gray mud.
> My body is aching, breaking and shaking
> With mud----gray mud.
> No depth am I sounding, I'm drowning, I'm drowning
> In MUD!---MUD!---MUD!---[18]

In spite of mud, isolation and several other difficulties, the 857 settled into camp and began work in earnest on Caddo Lake State Park completing the well for their new camp. While the corpsmen worked, though, Emergency Conservation Work administrators struggled to overcome one of those other difficulties, the efforts of area land owners to retain mineral rights to property closely bordering park lands. Recent oil discoveries in Rhodessa, Louisiana, a few miles northeast of the park site led property owners to file "protect notices" on the project superintendent.[19] About 400 oil wells out of over 600 drilled since 1907 were still pumping in the lake on the Louisiana side. On the Texas side several resort and fishing camps continued operations quite near park boundaries. Leaders from Marion and Harrison counties who had been enthusiastic to begin the park project were now feuding about handing over acreage adjacent to the park boundaries. The situation was so tense that administrators tried to keep each group of county leaders from learning of agreements made with the other.[20] Regional Emergency Conservation Work administrators arranged separate agreements and finally gained enough land by spring, 1935, to protect the Caddo project site where company 857 had continued to work.

8.1 Caddo Lake State Park Entry Pillar. Courtesy Texas Parks and Wildlife Department.

Acting Superintendent, W.B. Edwards, reported in May 1935 that the Company had completed most of the projects begun by Company 889 and were completing several others. Roadways and bridges were in use. The entrance gate with dual rock pillars was nicely finished with a small visitors' center ready for use. The main building was in use and overnight cabins, picnic areas, camp sites and rest room facilities were well along their way. This progress was leading to increasing use of the Park by North East Texans and residents from surrounding states.[21] At the end of September our poet, Joe Westbrook, now promoted to Acting Superintendent, used his quarterly report to extol the educational and recreational activities in the camp. Baseball, basketball and football teams were organized. Corpsmen learned to type and attended carpentry, mechanics and music classes. They formed a camp band and invited young women from the area–with, of course, their chaperones – to camp dances.[22] Though some work was still to be done, in about one year, this CCC Company had created a state park for use by residents of Texas, and beyond.

8.2   CCC Company 857 Camp Band. Courtesy National Archives and Records Administration.

By the end of 1935, Co. 857 had been transferred to Paris State Park, with a side camp of about 30 corpsmen left working at Caddo. Residents of Lamar County, where Paris State Park was located, welcomed the corpsmen to their Crook Lake site. Unfortunately, local and county officials refused to transfer their lakeside land to the State Parks Board since CCC-built swimming facilities would be open to all on an integrated basis.[23] The issues of racial discrimination and the place of African Americans and other minorities in the CCC haunted the program throughout its existence. Legislation creating the CCC "stipulated no discrimination on the basis of race. . ." Yet, "African American Corpsmen faced segregation, discrimination and hostility within the CCC and from nearby white communities."[24]

This "no discrimination on the basis of race" statement was part of an amendment to the original legislation offered by the only African American member of the U.S. House at the time, Oscar De Priest (R, Ill.). The congressman's amendment particularly focused on equal pay and that began to create a few cracks in the Jim Crow, low wage, slave-like system.[25] One Pennsylvania financier complained to a fellow DuPont board member: "Five Negroes on my place in South Carolina refused work this spring. . . . A cook on my houseboat at Fort Myers quit because the government was paying him a dollar an hour as a painter."[26] The CCC, though, was finally forced to segregate its companies in 1935.[27] The national office ordered all CCC camps in the south to be strictly segregated.[28]

Texas only reluctantly enrolled African Americans in the CCC and even if they were part of otherwise white companies, they were relegated to cooking and cleaning duties and segregated from the rest of the company.[29] State Director Neal Guy encouraged all eligible young men to apply, but a quota system prevented African Americans from obtaining many positions. Pressure from officials in Texas, almost all white, limited acceptance of black applicants to the number of vacancies in already established African American companies.[30] The same leaders then hesitated to accept those companies into their communities. Where such companies were placed, however, few problems were reported and when the camps were discontinued those same leaders complained loudly.[31]

Interestingly, the Harrison County Colored Country Club was among the original donors of land for the Caddo project. The club was not a golf course but a lakeside recreation center for African American residents.[32] Members believed they would have general, if not full, access to the state park. Such access was finally gained, but the struggle took more than two generations. State officials spent the next 25 years working to legislate and solidify a system of "separate but equal" segregation. In 1951 State Senator Warren McDonald of Tyler introduced legislation that would convert Caddo State Park "for Negro use only."[33] That bill did not withstand court review, but fully inclusive policies were not legally established until the Federal Civil Rights Act of 1964. At Caddo, their practice would wait another decade.

As it happened, Company 857 spent little time at the Paris camp. About 60 corpsmen were assigned to work on the CCC exhibit at the Texas Centennial in Dallas, but the majority of 857 corpsmen was soon returned to Caddo Lake. Though their official assignment was to SP-56 near Paris, the company remained at the Caddo site until the project was complete.[34] The office of Emergency Conservation Work sent written notice of its intention to transfer title of all CCC buildings at Caddo Lake to the Texas State Parks Board on April 17, 1937. Given the reality of paperwork the transfer did not become official until September 29. The remnants of Company 857 cleaned up, packed up and finally moved out in early November.[35] This site was now officially Caddo Lake State Park and still attracts visitors 80 years later.

Several CCC companies continued work on projects across Texas for five more years. Perhaps the last CCC camp in the country was in Texas. In his book on FDR and land conservation, Douglas Brinkley writes, "On August 11, 1942, the last CCC boys, eighty-two members of Veterans' Company 3822 in Goliad, Texas – a camp the first lady once visited – were dismissed."[36] A more poignant closing thought was offered from Alaska by newsletter editor Abraham H. Cohen. In one of his final issues of *The Alaskan*, Cohen took his cue from Abraham Lincoln and wrote this tribute to the CCC boys. "Little will the world remember what we say here [but] present and future generations can never forget what they are doing here."[37] Abraham Cohen's vision of a long-term memory of the work of the Civilian Conservation Corps and continued recognition of the significant positive impact of the New Deal in Texas and beyond may or may not prove true. That responsibility falls to historians to continue searching the record and to tell those stories to the coming generations.

Notes and Acknowledgments

An earlier version of this paper was presented for the New Deal Session at the East Texas Historical Association meeting in Galveston, October 12, 2017. Jennifer Carpenter and Cynthia Brandimarte of Texas Parks and Wildlife were a significant help in this project. Cynthia's book, *Texas State Parks and the CCC*, got me started and Jennifer provided primary source documents from Parks and Wildlife files. Their help has been essential to this paper. I also thank my friend, Dan K. Utley, who connected me with several critical sources.

[1] Jesse I. Carter, Press release for the Caddo Lake State Park dedication, June 1934, in Caddo Lake State Park, the First Sixty Years, 1934-1994, Gail Beil & others, Marshall, Texas: *News Messenger*, 1994, np. Courtesy Texas Parks and Wildlife Department.

[2] Progressive Merchants of Marshall, Texas, "Dedication of Caddo Lake State Park near Marshall, Texas" program for the event, July 4, 1934, Courtesy of TPWD.

[3] Cynthia Brandimarte, *Texas State Parks and the CCC: The Legacy of the Civilian Conservation Corps*, College Station: Texas A&M University Press, 2013, p. 13.

[4] Walter L. Harris. "Margie E. Neal: The First Woman Senator in Texas," *East Texas Historical Journal*, Vol. XI No. 1 (Spring, 1973) pp. 40-50.

[5] James Wright Steely, *Parks for Texas: Enduring Landscapes of the New Deal*, Austin: University of Texas Press, 1999, pp. 5-6.

[6] Douglas Brinkley, *Rightful Heritage: Franklin D. Roosevelt and the Land of America*, New York: HarperCollins, 2016, p. 371.

[7] Brandimarte, p. xiii.

[8] Steely, p. 29.

[9] Steely, p. 203.

[10] Caddo Lake State Park Files, National Park Service CCC Papers, Group 79, Boxes 51-52, National Archives and Records Administration, Denver, p. 61. Courtesy TPWD.

[11] Caddo Files, p. 63.

[12] Carter Press Release.

[13] Steely, p. 79.

[14] Caddo Files, p. 64.

[15] Caddo Files, p. 38.

[16] Harold L. Buckles, Ed. *The 857 Log*, Nov. 1933 – Jan. 1935, III/1, p. 1, via the Center for Research Libraries, Courtesy TPWD.

[17] Buckles, III/1, p. 2.

[18] Buckles, III/4, p. 2.

[19] Caddo Files, p. 30.

[20] Caddo Files, p. 35.

[21] Caddo Files, pp. 50-52.

[22] Caddo Files, pp. 53-54.

[23] Steely, p. 222.

[24] Olin Cole Jr. *The African American Experience in the Civilian Conservation Corps*, Gainesville, University Press of Florida, 1999, p. 1.

[25] John A. Salmond, *The Civilian Conservation Corps, 1933-1942: A New Deal Case Study*, Durham, NC: Duke University Press, 1967, p. 23.

[26] Kim Phillips-Fein, *Invisible Hands: The Businessmen's Crusade against the New Deal*, New York: W.W. Norton, 2009, pp. 4-5.

[27] Brandimarte, p. 52.

[28] Kenneth E. Hendrickson Jr. "Replenishing the Soil and Soul of Texas: The Civilian Conservation Corps in the Lone Star State as an Example of State-Federal Work Relief during the Great Depression," Faculty Papers, Series 2, Vol. 1, Wichita Falls, Texas: Midwestern State University, 1974-1975, p. 811. Courtesy of Dan Utley.

[29] Mary L. Wilson, "Texans and the Civilian Conservation Corps: Personal Memories, The *Southwestern Historical Quarterly*, Vol 117, No. 2 (October 2013) pp. 144-163.

[30] William J. Brophy, "Black Texans and the New Deal" in *The Depression in the Southwest*, Donald W. Whisenhunt, Ed. Port Washington, NY, National University Publications, 1980, pp. 120-21.

[31] Hendrickson, p. 812.

[32] Steely, p. 30.

[33] Dan K. Utley with Stanley O. Graves, *Links to the Past: The Hidden History on Texas Golf Courses*, College Station: Texas A&M University Press, 2018, pp. 220 & 222. Utley references the Corsicana *Daily Sun*, and the *Valley Morning Star* (Harlingen) April 6, 1951.

[34] Steely, p. 222.

[35] Caddo Files, pp. 203ff.

[36] Brinkley, p. 526.

[37] Alfred Emile Cornebise, *The CCC Chronicles:* Camp Newsletters of the Civilian Conservation Corps, 1933-1942, Jefferson: Pictorial Histories Publishing Co. 1980, p. 1.

The New Deal in Cass County, Texas, 1933-1943

Brenda Taylor Matthews

9.1 *The Last Crop.* (see cover image) Photo by the author.

In Cass County, Texas, atop the postmaster's door, *The Last Crop* mural topped off a decade of New Deal expenditures meant to address hunger, unemployment, poor health, and poverty caused by the Great Depression. Painted on canvas in San Francisco and installed by the artist Victor Arnautoff in the new Linden post office building in September 1939, *The Last Crop* depicted the final Black cotton pickers before automation supplanted their labor. The landowner's bucolic home on the horizon and the sharecropper's drought-worn dogtrot on the distant right reflected Arnautoff's favorite theme, the juxtaposition of wealth and poverty. A refugee of the Russian Revolution, Arnautoff attended the California School of Fine Arts between 1925 and 1929 and subsequently worked with Diego Rivera in Mexico, supervising the completion of the Mexican's famous murals at the National Palace in Cuernavaca in late 1930. Arnautoff returned to San Francisco in the summer of 1931 just as unemployment reached eighteen percent. Within two years, he became an important influence in the city's art community and was selected as one of the twenty-five artists for the new Coit Tower. Built by the estate of a Lillie Hitchcock Coit as part of city beautification, the tower's interior was to illustrate contemporary California with art funded by the Treasury Department's Section of Fine Arts. This placed Arnautoff on the New Deal relief payroll. The Linden mural, described by the postmaster as "an excellent piece of work and is admired by everyone," was one of Arnautoff's eight government mural contracts. Like so many in the Depression, artists too struggled to house and feed their families, and Arnautoff looked to the newly elected Franklin Delano Roosevelt to fulfill his campaign promises.[1]

Addressing an anxious yet hopeful nation on inauguration day 1933, President Franklin Roosevelt informed his listeners that "We must act; we must act quickly." With FDR's urging, Congress in the next 100 days passed New Deal legislation to address the Depression's unemployment and resulting ills. Northeastern Texas Cass County, organized in 1846 out of Bowie County, was a recipient of most of these New Deal experiments. The county seat, Linden, was centered in the heavily soft and hard-wood forested landscape of rolling hills. Although only twenty-one to thirty percent of the county was prime farmland, its forty-seven inches of rainfall and long growing season was attractive in the 1840s as it was close to Jefferson, Texas, shipping port. By 1860, cotton, corn, and hog production dominated as the Texas and Pacific and the East Line and Red River Railways spurred growth in Atlanta, Queen City, Hughes Spring, and Linden. Despite farm price insecurity, three-quarters of the croplands were planted in cotton and corn through the 1920s and fifty-seven percent of workers remained in agriculture, with sixty-one percent of those tenants in 1930. Mules and horses carried people and goods until the 1940s when automobiles and road building improved movement.[2]

With most Cass County employment in agriculture, the crash on October 29, 1929, made little initial impact. The next issue of the *Cass County Sun* newspaper on November 5th ran only a two-inch column on page two's "News Review of Current Events" noting the "wildest scenes the New York stock exchange has ever known." The county was already in financial difficulty from the post-World War cotton collapse with Egypt and India again supplying cotton to Europe and American producers using synthetics. Bringing twenty cents per pound in 1925, prices fell to less than ten cents the next year. In the *Cass County Sun*, October 30, 1928, the county agent urged farmers to create a bonded warehouse and grow a better staple cotton. Nevertheless, as farmers did during the whole of the previous century when prices fell, they just planted more. In 1929, over sixty percent of the county's arable land, 123,753 acres, was in cotton, producing a record 37,508 bales. Moreover, farm values fell by half from 1920 to 1930, from $2,504 to $1,554. With the widening of the Depression, farm poverty increased nationwide so that by June 1935 farmers made up over thirty percent of Federal Emergency Relief Administration (FERA) cases. *There is no reason to believe that Cass County farmers fared any better.*[3]

How to address rural poverty became a central issue for Roosevelt's administration. Emergency funds directly to the states, public works projects providing both jobs and community improvement, adequate shelter, and new schools all became a part of the equation of FDR's "good earth" of rural living. The day after the inauguration FDR approved relief funds for seven states, and on May 12 he signed the Federal Emergency Relief Act of 1933. The bill channeled $500 million left over from Hoover's Reconstruction Finance Corporation (RFC) to direct aid. Progressive social work theorist and FERA Administrator Harry L. Hopkins insisted on cash relief instead of demeaning donations of food and clothing. Hopkins' "Unemployment Relief Census" that summer revealed fifteen million persons, or twelve percent of the population, dependent on relief funds, including one million farm families. Working through state and local entities FERA distributed monies to a myriad of programs. These included teachers for Adult Education and nursery schools, all-weather farm to market roads, sidewalks and culverts in small towns, and wages to keep libraries open. Additionally, FERA planned to improve other parts of civic life by building schools, courthouses, and waterworks, as well as furnishing public health needs. "Production for use" projects whereby goods went only to relief clients, included sewing rooms, community gardens, canning, and mattress making and began operation quickly in Linden County. One farm rehabilitation grant of $75 bought stock, cows and pigs and harnesses, tools, and feed.[4]

Funneling funds through state emergency entities however slowed down aid. The continuing job loss and oncoming winter spurred Roosevelt's creation by executive order in November the Civil Works Administration (CWA) to speed up employment. Authorized through March 1, 1934, the CWA continued FERA's "economically and socially desirable" community improvement projects in Cass County. A November grant of $1500 continued paying wages for a wood-cutting program. Also, an announcement in the Atlanta *Citizens Journal* on November 30, 1933, assured workers providing teams and trucks on RFC payrolls were continued payment. Cass County Civil Works administrator W.A. Barber made multiple applications as early as November 11 to state relief administrator Colonel Lawrence Westbrook for road improvements. Initial monies for all four precincts totaled $149,000 for repairing culverts, increasing drainage, and grading and graveling roads for year-around access. The county's largest town, Atlanta, needed $32,000 for street upgrades in a December application, while one of the smallest communities, Bloomburg, asked for only a fourth of that for graveling roads. In January, the state approved almost $4000 to gravel the important mail and school route between Douglasville,

Casseta in northwest Cass County, and Linden.[5]

Barber also made appeals for a multitude of school enhancements. A December 1 application for improving the Atlanta school grounds by grading the site, planting trees and shrubs, and building a rock bridge for $1680 made its way to the state office. In January other schools followed suit. The Sardis school, twelve miles west of Linden, asked for $192 to level its grounds while six miles south of Hughes Spring the Turkey Creek school wanted $176.20 to improve the well and school grounds, paint the building, and build swings, see-saws and steps. Linden needed extensive work on its high school, including grading and leveling of tennis, volley ball, and basket-ball courts and the football field and steps for the bleachers, amounting to $1971.30 of which $1872 state officials approved. Finally, in February, the Atlanta high school requested $898.02 to augment their locally raised $1647.84 to build a fine arts building. On August 10, 1934, a 175-piece band and local officials dedicated the fourteen practice rooms and large auditorium built with Atlanta-made bricks and CWA and FERA labor.[6]

Education and library projects also received funds. The Atlanta library hired Onie Willis in January to work five days a week from two to five and hired staff to catalogue materials for a total of $160. Linden officials also applied for library funds of $120 and CWA approved $480 for teaching adults "fundamental subjects" and another $924 for general education for the unemployed in December and January. Superintendent of Schools, Otha King Miles, also used monies to extend the school year in Rocky Point and in Holly Springs. Additionally, the district received $300 to score standardized tests given to ten thousand county students in February 1934.[7]

Operating concurrent with Harry Hopkins' FERA, Roosevelt's National Industrial Recovery Act (NIRA), signed on June 17, 1933, attempted to assist industry. Title I involved "codes of fair competition." Title II, more important for rural Cass County, focused on construction jobs through Secretary of the Interior Harold Ickes' Public Works Administration (PWA) with its $3.3 billion federal money and matching state funds. Known best for its large-scale construction, it continued many of the smaller CWA projects. CWA had granted the county's sewing rooms $1600 for fabric and wages of thirty-five cents up to fifteen hours per week in February 1934. According to an *Atlanta Citizens Journal* December 1935 issue, the PWA employed sixty-nine women in the sewing rooms in Linden, Hughes Spring, Atlanta, and Marietta.[8]

9.2 Cass County Courthouse, 1934. Charlene Wiley Morris History Collection, with permission from Sue Morris Lazara.

It was the PWA monies, however, that Cass County applied for when fire tore into its antebellum courthouse on August 9th. Built with four hundred thousand local bricks by slave labor in 1861, it replaced an 1854 frame courthouse. Builders expanded the Greek revival structure in 1905, adding Victorian touches and a cupola. In 1917, commissioners contracted with the Texarkana firm Witt, Siebert, Moore, and Halsey to expand and bring classical elements back to the facades. Architect Stewart Moore and engineer Fred Halsey gave the court house north and south portico entrances with 2-story Doric columns and east and west curved staircases. Unfortunately, sixteen years later just before noon on a Saturday, a fire in the judge's chambers spread quickly, burning all courtroom furnishings on the second floor. Without a water system in place, locals passed buckets to quash the flames and carried county records to safety. Nevertheless, flames destroyed the top floor before Jefferson's or Atlanta's fire departments arrived with pumping trucks. Cass County's United States Congressman, Wright Patman, quickly routed a $38,000 packet for the courthouse through the PWA. Patman, born near Hughes Springs, entered Congress emphasizing southern poverty, inequality of wealth, and farm relief, becoming a fervent New Deal supporter. Without Moore, the architect firm Witt, Siebert, and Halsey added a third floor. E.L. Steck Company furnished new courtroom furnishings for $5,448.51. The county accepted the final work from the contractors on January 14, 1935.[9]

9.3 Linden Water Tower, Cass County, Texas. Photo by author.

In addition to the Cass County courthouse, Congressman Patman wrote in his *Cass County Sun* "Weekly Letter" on Tuesday, August 28, 1934, the First Congressional District had secured "as many loans" as any other in the country, excepting those that had large projects such as dams, with fourteen out of thirty-three applications already appropriated. The loans totaled $703,100, with thirty percent, or $210, 930, being grants. These and subsequent Washington monies secured Patman's seat for the next thirty years. Approved were a new school for the small community of Avinger for $3,300 and a $14,000 larger six-classroom school plus auditorium made of fourteen thousand county-made bricks in Marietta. Road building included completion of Highway 47 and 49 and the Douglassville-Atlanta route. Patman also announced the funding of two major waterworks projects, one for Hughes Springs at $62,000 and one for Linden. The $50,000 Linden loan provided a new well, a 50,000-gallon elevated storage tank, and a sewage system. Construction moved quickly with Kilgore contractor O.L. Crigler receiving $32,745 to lay the pipes and dig the pool in January. A new well and pump were let for an additional $8,000. Work neared completion in October when the *Cass County Sun* informed citizens to sign up for their new meters.[10]

Unfortunately, opposition to relief programs by those on the left and the right led to retrenchment in FERA and a refocus on large-scale public works programs for PWA. Critics on the left felt the president was not doing enough, whereas those on the right opposed creeping government regulation of markets, involvement in people's private lives and socialism. Therefore, Roosevelt's new Works Progress Administration (WPA), created by executive order on May 6, stepped into job generation, spending over $285 million in Texas from 1935 to 1942. WPA divided Patman's First Congressional constituencies into two districts, with Cass County in District 1 headquartered in Marshall, thirty miles to the south. The focus remained on public projects with road applications for widening, grading, and resurfacing, as well as eliminating traffic hazards. Similarly, the WPA continued school improvements. In February 1935, WPA labor painted the Cornett School as well as beautified the grounds; later in November, Queen City hired twenty-one men to build a three-room brick veneer class-room building and a two-room shop. Originally submitted to the PWA, Atlanta schools built a new school for white children in 1936. Hardy Brothers Construction completed the six-room school in 120 days. Later, in 1939, Bivins Consolidated School District received monies to tear down two existing structures and build new classrooms. The small town of Bloomburg constructed a new school in 1941, eight years after applying first for CWA monies. Needing additional space, the county erected an office building in 1939, with the health department, Farm Security Administration, and Agricultural Adjustment Administration moving in on October 12th.[11]

Although coming to Cass County relatively late, the Civilian Conservation Corps (CCC), created by congress on March 31, 1933, was meant to alleviate young male unemployment. The May 30, 1935, Atlanta *Citizens Journal* announced twelve acres of land owned by Cal Williams near Linden to be the site of a CCC camp for the district. Work began on July 25, when six cars of materials to build portable wood buildings arrived. Initial workers included junior enrollees, eight to twenty-five; veterans of the World War; and sixteen experienced men to fill positions such as mechanic or blacksmith. The CCC began with soil conservation. After approving a farmer's plan, the CCC would map the farm and the Soil Conservation Service make an erosion survey. Work typically included terrace building and sodding with oats or Bermuda grass. The camp was augmented in May 1937, when Company 1814 transferred to Camp P-90. The unit built thirty-five miles of roads, connected forest service towers with 147 miles of telephone lines, reforested, and fought fires with the Texas Forest Service. By the end of the 1939, the CCC troops had completed all their authorized work and the camp closed on September 28.[12]

Although these agencies and projects had assisted with the jobs in construction, the New Deal also addressed farm conditions. Secretary of Agriculture Henry Wallace and brain trvust advisor Rexford Tugwell suggested a "domestic allotment" to reduce production. The resulting May 12, 1933, legislation, the Agricultural Adjustment Act (AAA) also came to Cass County with local farmers agreeing to thirty percent crop reduction contracts. Subsequently, county agent M.D. Jaynes held a June meeting at Linden, assigning sixty-five committees appointed by A&M College to inspect cotton acreage. In January, CWA funding of $960 paid for clerical help to follow up on the 1934 and 1935 contracts. The new Resettlement Administration (RA) resettled families from destitute land and loaned monies for land and equipment. After Roosevelt's victory in November, the emboldened Congress passed the Bankhead-Jones Farm Tenant Act creating the Farm Security Administration (FSA) to assist southern poor and a second, modified, AAA in 1938 stepped back into commodity subsidies. Allotment recipients in Cass County, like many elsewhere, forced tenants and sharecroppers off the land and over the next decade farm size grew from an average of sixty-eight to ninety-two acres. By 1940, more than fifty percent of farmers in Cass County were proprietors.[13]

Health issues impacted farmers as much as low crop prices and unemployment. Although the Great War had influenced the United States Public Health Service, (USPHS) to instigate programs such as malaria control, sanitary projects, and venereal campaigns, their influence varied widely by region and little progress was made throughout the twenties as farm areas continued their downward slide. Subsequently, New Deal agencies such as the CWA, the Interior Department's Division of Subsistence Homestead, Rexford Tugwell's 1935 Resettlement Administration, and the 1937 FSA each found that a farmer's health impacted his success. A WPA monograph, *The Plantation South*, 1934-1937, blamed inadequate shelter, poor or non-existent sanitation, deficient diet, and lack of education for the high rates of illness in the rural south. Remote areas also operated under the handicap of fewer public health control measures and agencies. A survey of forty counties in various southern states showed that only one-third had the ability to contain the simplest of contagious childhood diseases.[14]

Cass County, however, again benefitted from Wright Patman's efforts. As a state congressman and then again in the U.S. House, Patman steered aid to the county for diseases such as pellagra, malaria, and syphilis and sanitation improvement. Ahead of the curve, as in 1930 most Texas counties did not have a health unit, county commissioners hired general practitioner and pharmacist Dr. O. R. Taylor in January 1931 to serve as health officer. In June the county applied to the USPHS for funds to augment their $85 for public health education, immunizations, malaria and hookworm control, and general sanitation. The new health committee asked for funds for a fulltime health officer, nurse, secretary, and inspectors. The CWA authorized the hiring of nurse Ruth McCaskill in February 1934.[15]

9.4.   Rock wall built by WPA in Linden. Photo by author.

The unit focused on several sanitation related diseases. To eliminate hookworm, the CWA funded county health sanitary engineer Dan T. Bartlett's installation of fifty-two pit privies and the sale of two hundred more in early 1934. Cost was $12.50 for the complete unit, but only $5.50 for the slab for an existing outhouse. The health unit applied to the WPA in 1938 for over $13,000 to augment the $10,067 county funds to construct additional privies and septic systems. As part of the hookworm campaign, a *Cass County Sun* article in March 1939 urged Cass County's rural population over the next several years to "do away" with surface outhouses. Work continued that summer with thirty-two privies installed in June and over fifty more orders for July. To address malaria control, in 1939 WPA funds eliminated breeding pools in Linden and Hughes Springs, lining multiple ditches with concrete and rock walls. The WPA continued to fight malaria with a $19,317 grant in September 1940.[16]

Despite these efforts and FSA medical assistance to its loan recipients, health problems persisted. The declaration of war in 1941 revealed severe draftee deficiencies. Rural inductees had a higher rejection rate than urban males, with "farmers and farm managers" having the highest at 56.4 percent. As part of post-war planning, the FSA launched an "experimental medical program." One of two in Texas, and only one of six nationwide, the Cass County Rural Health Association had characteristics that met several criteria, including being predominantly rural and medical professionals willing to participate in cooperative medicine. The Cass County Agricultural Planning Committee reported ninety-percent of school children had some defect and at least twenty percent were malnourished in 1939 and 1940. The county had 255 active tuberculosis patients and the Selective Service Board had rejected 23.3 percent of men examined. Required by the FSA, Cass County farm families incorporated a health association in June 1942 and elected a board of directors to negotiate agreements with medical professionals.[17]

The association determined membership dues upon a fee per service basis with families paying based on their income up to $50 annually. The FSA supplemented costs over the next two years with a $96,350 grant, covering care of a general practitioner, surgeons, and specialists; diagnostic and therapeutic procedures in conjunction with hospitalization; prescription drugs; and dental care. By the end of fiscal year 1942, Cass County had the largest membership with over twenty-four hundred families enrolled. Unfortunately, the next year, eleven hundred families cited cost as the reason for their non-enrollment, with only five hundred new families enrolled. When the FSA subsidies ended in 1946 with the agency's demise, county officials hoped to continue some form of medical services through a health center.[18]

Cass County in rural northeastern Texas was not unique in receiving New Deal assistance. From 1936 to 1943, Texas received over $300 million in WPA funds. Almost forty percent of those dollars went to road improvement and construction. Water and sewage systems received six percent and sanitation two percent with eleven percent going to buildings. Cass County received funds for projects in each of these areas. Highways and farm to market roads were improved for the new mode of car and truck transportation; a new courthouse and county annex as well as schools were constructed; and Hughes Springs' and Linden's waterworks and sanitation projects across the county benefitted. Although often criticized as "make work" and analyzed by scholars as not having ended the Depression, New Deal projects injected needed dollars into bereft rural communities and left tangible remains behind. A restored antebellum courthouse, an historic water tower, a school preservation project, and a mural all remain to remind Cass County residents of the New Deal, FDR's grand experiment.

Notes and Acknowledgments

I wish to thank local Cass County historian Kay Stephens, grand-daughter of Linden doctor O.R. Taylor, for assisting me with document retrieval in the county archives, giving me a tour of Linden's New Deal projects, and buying me lunch in a café on the Linden square. Her hospitality made a research trip to Linden in June 2018 thoroughly enjoyable. Additionally, *The Historic Cass County Courthouse* author Sue Morris Lazara graciously shared a photograph taken by her mother, Charlene Wiley Morris. Her insight on Linden history rounded out my vision of 1930s Cass County.

[1] One of a 106 artworks in sixty-nine Texas post offices, sources alternately referred to it as Cotton Pickers, probably confused with artist's later lithograph. Arnautoff also painted a mural, *Good Technique-Good Harvest*, featuring cotton pickers for the College Station Post Office, but it was destroyed during a renovation. Robert W. Cherny, *Victor Arnautoff and the Politics of Art* (Urbana: University of Illinois Press, 2017), 43-57, 65-75, 81-3, 125, 189; Philip Parisi, *The Texas Post Office Murals* (College Station: Texas A&M University Press, 2004), 3-5, 77-8.

[2] Franklin D. Roosevelt, *Looking Forward* (New York: John Day, 1933), 265; Brenda Jeanette Taylor (Matthews), "The Farm Security Administration: Meeting Rural Health Needs in the South, 1933-1946" (Ph.D. diss., Texas Christian University, 1994), 41-42; *Handbook of Texas Online*, Cecil Harper, Jr., "Cass County," 2-14, accessed June 08, 2017, http://www.tshaonline.org/handbook/online/articles/hcc07; Texas Legislature named new county after ardent supporter of annexation, Michigan Senator Lewis Cass. During the Civil War, the state rejected the name, as Cass was born in New Hampshire, and rechristened the county Davis after the Confederate president. The county reverted to Cass in 1871. Sue Morris Lazara, *The Historic Cass County Courthouse* (Linden, Texas: Linden Garden Club, 2012), 9, 54-55; Keith J. Volanto, *Texas, Cotton, and the New Deal* (College Station, Texas: A&M Press, 2005), 6.

[3] John Kenneth Galbraith, *The Great Crash, 1929* (Boston: Houghton Mifflin Company, 1988), xi-xviii, 11; The *Cass County Sun* (Linden, Texas) Portal of Texas History, October 30, 1928. The crash news came from the Chicago's Western Newspaper Union. November 5, 1929 (hereafter *Sun*); Harper, *Handbook, 12; American bankers hesitant to provide loans to Europe to buy American products effected exports of cotton*. Volanto, 12-14; *Works Progress Administration, Division of Social Research, Farmers on Relief and Rehabilitation*, by Berta Asch and A.R. Mangus (Washington, D.C.: GPO, 1937), 4, also in Taylor, 42.

[4] President Hoover signed the Emergency Relief and Construction Act of 1932 as a concession to relief needs. This bill allowed the RFC to lend up

to $300 million to the states for relief to be repaid in June 1935. Woefully inadequate, only $30 million was spent on relief by the end of the year despite increasing requests for funds. After the creation of FERA, the RFC became the funnel for federal relief funds. Arthur M. Schlesinger, Jr., *The Age of Roosevelt, Vol.1, Crisis of the Old Order* (Boston: Houghton Mifflin Company, 1957), 397, 241, also in Taylor, 40; By June 1933, the Cass County rural roads committee had solicited a million dollars for 168 miles of road from Westbrook. *Atlanta Citizen's Journal* (Atlanta, Texas), Atlanta Public Library and Portal of Texas History, June 22, 1933, May 3, 1934 (hereafter *Citizens*); Nick Taylor, *American Made: The Enduring Legacy of the WPA* (New York: Bantam Books, 2008), 69; Franklin D. Roosevelt, *The Public Papers and Addresses of Franklin D. Roosevelt*, Vol.1, *The Genesis of the New Deal: 1928-1932* (New York: Random House, 1938), 789-94, also in Taylor, 40; John F. Bauman and Thomas H. Coode, *In the Eye of the Depression* (DeKalb: Northern Illinois University, 1988), 5-9; Sidney Baldwin, *Poverty and Politics* (Chapel Hill: University of North Carolina Press, 1968), 60-62; Nancy E. Rose, *Put to Work: The WPA and Public Employment in the Great Depression* (New York: Monthly Review Press, 2009), 25-55.

[5] The CWA was under the authority of National Industrial Recovery Administration and defunded by May 1934 with project funding reverting to FERA. Rose, 37-45; "Application for Civil Works Project, Wood Cutting," (hereafter CWA) Project Number (hereafter #) 1558, Cass County, Texas, (Reel 253) (hereafter R); "WPA Project Proposal for Roads," (hereafter WPA) #15317 (R B552); "WPA for highway improvements," #16860 (R C302); "CWA for Atlanta school," #W1192 (R 7605), United States, Records of the Work Projects Administration and its Predecessors, Texas, 1931-1944, Record Group 69, Microfilm at Texas A&M University, College Station, Texas; *Sun*, January 9, 1934; *Citizens*, June 22, 1933.

[6] *Citizens*, November 30, 1933, January 11, 1934, August 9, 1934; Rose, 39-40; "CWA for school grounds," #4502; "CWA Linden high school improvements," #9647; "CWA Turkey Creek school," #9666; "CWA Atlanta schools fine arts building," #20250 (all on R 253).

[7] "CWA county library work," #6802; "CWA teaching of adult children," #9689; "CWA clerical help to file county records," #10173; "CWA teaching of unemployed and other adults," #10174; "CWA grading, scholastics, testing material," #10175 (all on R 253); *Citizens*, January 11, 1934.

[8] Baldwin, 62-3; Alonzo Hamby, *Man of Destiny: FDR and the Making of the American Century* (New York: Basic Books, 2015), 186; Citizens, February 8, 1934, December 5, 1935; The sewing rooms were successful enough that the PWA continued to fund them in December 1939. *Sun*, December 14, 1939.

[9] The courthouse was completed a month after secession. Lazara, 2, 38-9,

48, 60-72; Moore apprenticed with Fort Worth architects Marshall Sanguinet and Carl Staats. Lazara, 73; Citizens, August 24, 1933; Nancy Beck Young, *Wright Patman: Populism, Liberalism, and the American Dream* (Dallas: SMU Press, 2000), 1-25; *Sun*, March 13, 1934, August 7, 1934; Dallas builder F.A. Mote receiving general and electrical contracts and a Texarkana company the plumbing contract on June 15, 1934. Cass County Commissioners Court Minutes (hereafter Commissioners), Cass County Courthouse, Linden, Texas, October 9, 1933, June 15, 1934, August 21, 1934, January 14, 1935; Stewart Moore had left Texarkana to return to Fort Worth and Sanguinet and Staats. The architecture firm designed buildings from western Texas to Missouri. Under the Texas Historic Courthouse Preservation Program, the community restored the courthouse to its 1934 appearance and rededicated it in 2012. Lazara, i-iii, 70-3.

[10] *Sun*, January 30, 1934, August 28, 1934, October 2, 1934, October 9, 1934, February 14, 1935; Citizens, April 12, 1934; Dr. Hamilton J. Avinger donated land for the East Line and Red River Railroad and founded the community around 1876 nine miles southwest of Hughes Springs. Texas State Historical Commission Marker 1471; "WPA highway improvements," #16862, R C302; "Public Works Administration (hereafter PWA) Waterworks improvements Hughes Springs," #W2059, R 7480. Hamby, 218-49; *Sun*, August 1, 1935; Jane Warner Rogers, "WPA Pr

[11] Hamby, 218-49; *Sun*, August 1, 1935; Jane Warner Rogers, "WPA Professional and Service Projects in Texas" (M.A. thesis, University of Texas, 1976), 1-4; Citizens, February 7, 1935, November 7, 1935, October 12, 1939; Atlanta added to the school, renaming it Miller Grade School. The school was integrated in 1970 and closed in 1974. Texas State Historical Commission Marker 13424; "WPA County road improvements," #14471, R E252; "WPA Bloomburg school construction," #15029, R E256; "WPA County road improvements," #13319, R 289; "WPA Bivins school construction," #15185, R B551; "WPA County road improvements Hughes Springs," #15481, R B553.

[12] Organized in Fort Logan, Colorado, the company had more recently worked at camp P-71 at Groveton and at Austin's Zilker Park. *Sun*, July 18, 1935, July 25, 1935, January 5, 1939, October 5, 1939; *Citizens*, May 30, 1935, December 5, 1935.

[13] Roosevelt created the RA in May 1935 by executive order when AAA's work seemed insufficient. The U.S. Supreme Court ruled the AAA unconstitutional in January 1936 in U.S. v Butler over the processor tax used to shore up commodity prices. Hamby, 184-85, 248; Harper, 12; Commissioners, February 12, 1934; *Citizens*, June 29, 1933; "CWA clerical help for agriculture department," #13197, R 253.

[14] Taylor, 12; United States Congress, House of Representatives, Select

Committee of the House Committee on Agriculture to Investigate the Activities of the Farm Security Administration, Farm Security Administration, 78th Cong., May 11 to 28, 1943, 1621-22; Carl C. Taylor, ed., *Rural Life in the United States* (New York: Alfred A. Knopf, 1949), 157-58; Work Projects Administration, Division of Research, The Plantation South, 1934-1937, by William C. Holley (Washington, D.C.: Work Projects Administration, Division of Research, 1940), 60.

[15] Young, 37; Frederick D. Mott, *Rural Health and Medical Care* (New York: McGraw-Hill, 1948), 339-40; Dr. Taylor first practiced pharmacy, working until he could save money to attend medical school at Texas Christian University in Fort Worth. According to his grand-daughter Kay Stephens, the "country doctor" practiced forty years in Cass County. Commissioners, January 12, 1931, June 18, 1931; Citizens, February 1, 1934, December 13, 1934.

[16] *Citizens*, July 6, 1939, February 1, 1934, December 13, 1934; One wall built near the school still stands. *Sun*, July 20, 1939; "WPA Sanitation project, privies," #10785, R D280; "WPA combat malaria near Atlanta," #17241, R C305.

[17] Mott, 116-19; The USDA regional attorney assisted in writing the articles of incorporation and constitution or by-laws. They were to be reviewed then by the USDA Solicitor's Office in Washington. "Experimental Rural Health Program," 5, 13, March 1942, File: Newton County Agricultural Health Association, Box 349, E 7, Records of and Related to Cooperative Associations, 1935-1954, Farmer's Home Administration, Record Group 96, National Archives, Washington, D.C (hereafter Coop, RG 96).

[18] Mott, 416, 421; "Cass County Rural Health Service Audit 1943," File: Cass County Rural Health Service, Box 668, E 7, Coop, RG 96.

"We Patch Anything":
WPA Sewing Rooms in Fort Worth

Susan Allen Kline

The legacy of the WPA in Texas is still widely evident. Places such as Dallas' Dealey Plaza, Fort Worth's Farrington Field, the City Hall and Auditorium in Karnes City, the Comanche County Courthouse, Lamar Boulevard Bridge over Shoal Creek in Austin, and the native rubble-stone wall around Fort Bliss National Cemetery were all built by the WPA and still serve the communities for which they were created. Hundreds of other buildings, structures, and landscape improvements dot our cities and rural roads, while hundreds of others have been destroyed. Over the years, much focus has been given to projects such as these that engaged men working for the WPA. Less attention has been given to work performed by women WPA workers, perhaps in part because the majority of it was service-oriented and of an ephemeral nature.[1]

The WPA was created in 1935 as one of Franklin D. Roosevelt's New Deal-era relief programs. Originally called the Works Progress Administration, the name was changed to the Work Projects Administration in 1939. The WPA's regulations required that anyone employed by the agency had to be the economic head of his or her household. Generally, WPA employees had been referred (or certified) to the agency by local public relief programs. Whatever the type of project, whether it be construction (which employed three out of four WPA workers), education, recreation, health, sewing, and other professional and service projects, the federal government provided the majority of the funding with local sponsors, typically municipal or county governments, providing a small contribution usually in the form of materials or work space and utilities.[2]

During the New Deal, special work programs for women were first established through the Women's Division of the Federal Emergency Relief Administration in 1933. Projects included professional work such as clerical jobs or as librarians. Other work was domestic-related and included the creation of household goods, canning and the production of food, gardening, and the fabrication and repair of clothing. The latter program was the largest employer of women on the relief rolls across the country. Nationally, approximately seven percent of WPA workers were women engaged in sewing projects. A study conducted in Pittsburgh, Pennsylvania, in 1939 noted that nearly half of the women employed in sewing rooms had been unemployed for more than six years and approximately three-quarters had not been employed by the private sector on any jobs of consequence since 1935 (the year the WPA was organized).[3]

Far from being a program for women only in urban areas, sewing rooms could be found in small and large cities alike. In Texas, WPA sewing rooms were established in Alvarado, Dallas, Gladewater, Throckmorton, San Antonio, Texarkana, Brownsville, and Henrietta, among many other cities. In the early years of the program, the sponsor's portion of costs for the sewing room was very small compared to the federal allocation. For example, in 1935, the federal allocation for the sewing room in Henrietta was $3,300 and the local sponsor's cost was $139.[4] But even small amounts such as this could be a burden on local budgets.

The first sewing room in Fort Worth was established in 1935 and the program became the longest continually run WPA program in the city. For the first year it was entirely financed by the federal government. Because of this, the clothing that was produced could be distributed to nearby counties that did not have their own sewing rooms. The following year, the program was financed jointly by the city, county, and the federal government. The federal government provided funding for salaries, major supplies, and equipment. The city paid two-thirds of the other expenses and Tarrant County paid one-third. Because of this arrangement, all items produced by the sewing rooms stayed in the county.[5]

In the beginning, the women were paid $35 a month for 140 hours of work. Those who were promoted to floor ladies or cutters could make as much as $52 a month. The work began at 7:30 am. At one sewing room, a brief song service was held on the women's own time before the work day began. They worked eight-hour days until they had accumulated 70 hours at which time they would lay off for a few days and return for another 70 hours. This rotation made it possible for more women to work during the month. By 1939, there was a special shift for mothers who had to take their children to a nursery before their work day started.[6]

Women did not need to know how to sew to find work in the sewing rooms. The *Fort Worth Star-Telegram* noted "Women who have never done anything but chop cotton go there and learn to manipulate a needle and thread as effectively as they did a hoe." They were trained in a manner that emphasized the type of work a homemaker would do to provide for her own family. Those with little training started out hemming diapers. "Pretty soon they can turn out a neat shirt collar," stated the *Star-Telegram*, "and begin studying design and lines and color." If certain tasks such as making buttonholes proved to be difficult, they could go to special training classes. The women did not engage in piece work as each person was responsible for a garment from beginning to end. They averaged two to three garments a day (not including any trim work). All work was inspected and any piece not meeting sewing room standards was sent back to the offending seamstress.[7] Any woman with a special interest in design or an idea on trimming a garment was encouraged to do so. In 1937, it was noted that the 35 Mexican American women working at the sewing room were particularly skilled at handwork. The newspaper reported that "they are left to do the fine hemstitching and embroidery that goes on baby garments. No mother with a $10,000-a-year income would be ashamed of some of these baby clothes."[8]

10.1 Women who worked as floor ladies or cutters received higher wages than seamstresses. "Lays" such as these could consist of many layers of fabric requiring the use of power cutters. Courtesy "Texas and the WPA," (www.flickr.com).

Women in the sewing rooms were taught other things besides sewing. Illiterate women received basic educational training. At one point in the program, employees received an hour of instruction each day that covered such topics as home management, hygiene, budgeting and "food values," all as part of their work day. As a result of such instruction, the *Star-Telegram* noted "many families torn apart by poverty and poor management have been reunited." At one sewing room, 500 women received first aid training from the Red Cross on their own time.[9]

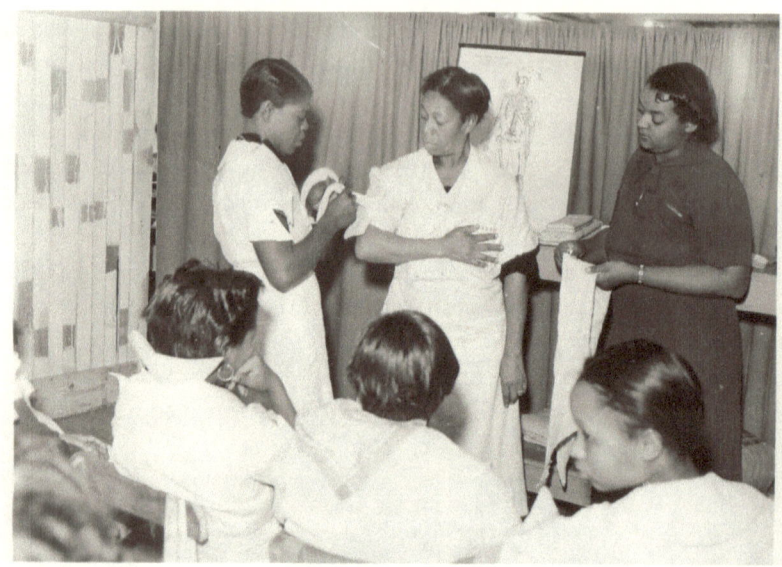

10.2 Sewing room workers received other forms of training including literacy, home management, hygiene and first aid as shown in this photograph. Courtesy "Texas and the WPA" (www.flickr.com).

A few men also found employment in the sewing rooms. Some of these jobs were upper-management positions such as superintendent of the program or cutting room supervisor. Others worked as firemen, watchmen, timekeepers, and porters. At least one African American man was employed as a porter, stacking the day's output on shelves.[10]

Through the years, sewing rooms were operated in various buildings. As in other larger cities in Texas, Fort Worth operated separate sewing rooms for African American and white women even though there was no such mandate at the federal level.[11] Evidence suggests that Mexican American women worked in the white sewing room.[12] In 1937, the sewing rooms, as well as the WPA's Home Economics Division, were moved into a former printing factory at 610 W. Daggett Street. This large, two-story brick building was centrally located just outside of the central business district, two blocks south of the Texas & Pacific Railway tracks. The sewing room for African Americans was located on the second floor. Previously, the two sewing rooms employed approximately 600 workers. It was anticipated that the new space could accommodate an additional 300 women.[13]

In early 1939, when the building at 610 W. Daggett Street was leased to H. J. Justin & Sons, the forerunner of today's Justin Boot Company, city and county officials were forced to find a new location for the sewing rooms. It proved difficult to find a building that could house the two segregated sewing rooms as well as the rest of the Home Economics Division. The city's land agent, P. J. Conway, told City Manager Dudley Lewis that he had "searched this town in every direction" and could not find an appropriate building that would suit these needs. The search was complicated by the fact that the county was not in a position to offer more money. As such, Conway suggested leasing two buildings, one at 13th and Jennings in the southern end of downtown and the Kingsbury Building at 1302 E. Lancaster for a combined rent of $60 a month.[14] The city even explored the option of constructing a building on city-owned land to house the WPA sewing room workers.[15] Because one suitable building could not be found, it was eventually decided that the Home Economic Division would move to the old City-County Hospital at 306 E. Third Street in downtown Fort Worth. That building had been recently vacated with the opening of a new city-county hospital on South Main Street that was constructed with funding from the Public Works Administration. Because the old hospital building was still owned by the county, local authorities would not have to pay rent as required with privately owned buildings. However, the white sewing room moved to the Parker-Browne Company Building, a three-story brick and concrete factory building located a mile east of downtown at 1212 E. Lancaster Avenue with easy access to public transportation. African American WPA sewing room workers were moved to the second floor of the Kingsbury Building, directly across the street to the east of the Parker-Browne Company Building. The monthly rent for the Parker-Browne Building was $250 per month. Rent for the space in the Kingsbury Building was $60 per month.[16]

Sewing rooms with hundreds of employees functioned best in buildings with large open spaces which likely accounts for the reason the old hospital building was not a suitable candidate for the sewing rooms. Factory buildings such as the one at 610 W. Daggett Street and the Parker-Browne Building were ideal. Their open floor space easily accommodated the many functions involved in the fabrication of clothing. Patterns were drawn by hand on large rolls of paper spread across flat surfaces. Multiple layers of fabric, sometimes as many as 200, could be laid out in a line (called a lay) on a long table. To make this process easier, Joseph H. Pyle, supervisor of one of the cutting rooms, designed a spreading machine that held the fabric as workers prepared to spread it on the table. The layers of fabric were cut with power cutters. Rows and rows of Singer sewing machines filled the assembly area. Handwork could be done while seated at long tables. In addition, the Parker-Browne Building's large windows helped to illuminate the interior and provided ventilation. Because there were few windows on the west side of the building, the women could work without facing the heat and glare of the afternoon sun.[17]

10.3   The open volume of the Parker-Browne Company Building was well suited for the tasks performed in the sewing rooms. Courtesy "Texas and the WPA" (www.flickr.com).

In 1939, it was reported that 1,000 women ranging in age from 19 to 65 worked at the Parker-Browne Building and 118 women worked at the sewing room for African American women. There were 340 sewing machines used in the white sewing room.[18] Each garment bore a WPA label with the inscription "Not to be sold." When finished, the items went to the surplus commodities depot and then distributed on order of county and city welfare case workers to needy individuals.[19] The sewing rooms were also called upon to make special items for other agencies or programs. For instance, Fort Worth's sewing room workers made drapes for a recreation center in Mineral Wells created for soldiers stationed at Camp Wolters.[20]

So as not to stigmatize recipients of WPA-made garments, care was taken to avoid the production of identical pieces of clothing with the exception of men's trousers, little boys' overalls, baby gowns, and diapers. According to a local newspaper, "Sewing room styles have improved so much in four years that a designing department functions now to give variety to stock patterns used. One pattern may be used for 50 dresses, but no two of the 50 will look alike when they are finished."[21]

From the inception of the program, the women who were employed in the sewing rooms took great pride in their work. The WPA was criticized frequently as being a "make work" program that sponsored projects of questionable worth. It was not uncommon for some to use the derisive phrase "We Piddle Around" when referring to the agency and its projects. Women working in the sewing room at the Used Clothes Depot knew their work was meaningful to so many and triumphantly proclaimed that the initials "WPA" stood for "We Patch Anything."[22]

The *Fort Worth Star-Telegram* published numerous favorable articles on the local sewing rooms as well as ones across the state. With such titles as "WPA Sewing Room Turns Out Expert Housekeepers," the newspaper reinforced the notion that the skills the women were learning applied only to their roles as homemakers. A photograph accompanying this article depicted a large room filled with women dressed in matching white smocks and seated behind their sewing machines, a scene that could have been mistaken for a garment factory.[23] The newspaper encouraged its readers to think of the less fortunate and to donate items for use in the sewing rooms, even those in less than perfect condition. "If you have any scraps at your house, buttons, yarn or baby clothes—anything you'd hesitate to peddle to the second-hand man or drop off at the rummage sale.... The sewing room workers can use them." The items could be dropped off at the home of Mrs. Everett Bass. Mrs. Bass did not work at a sewing room, but the program had become one of her "pet" interests.[24]

Readers of the newspaper were also encouraged to visit the sewing rooms to see for themselves the work accomplished by the WPA workers. In March 1937, the Home Economics Division, including the sewing room, held an open house so the public could learn about their work. According to the Star-Telegram, "That section of the public that knows nothing of the project likely will be amazed to learn of the Government-supported industry which gives employment to 900 women, white and colored." In May 1940, WPA projects in Fort Worth, including the white sewing room, participated in a nationwide "open house" to acquaint Americans with the "actual community values resulting from the operation of the professional and service division projects" of the agency.[25]

The plight of individual (white) workers and their families received sympathetic attention from the newspaper. A photograph of Emma Wuensch and her 20-year old daughter, Leona, tending her mother's injured leg, was prominently featured on the front page after she was accosted by a man while walking home from her job at a sewing room. The assailant took her purse containing her just-received paycheck of $17.50 for two-week's work, two nickels, and a streetcar token, "all she had left from her last check." Fortunately for Mrs. Wuensch and her two daughters, neighbors loaned her money until the WPA could reissue her check.[26] In 1936, an anonymous family was featured in the *Star-Telegram's* annual Christmas appeal for contributions to its Goodfellows Fund, established in 1912 as a charitable campaign to help impoverished children. The family included five children, a disabled father who was "unable to secure employment, even from the WPA," and a mother who earned $35 a month at the sewing room but at the time was not working there likely as a result of the shift rotations. In a letter to the fund, the family's seven-year old son stated that he needed shoes and clothes for school, noting that, "We would be proud to get toys, but would rather be prouder of clothes for mother can't buy them. She can hardly feed us on $35 a month."[27] The following year, an anonymous widow and her four young children were highlighted for the charity drive. The five lived in a miserable basement apartment on the city's north side that was heated by a smoky stove and its window patched with cardboard. While their mother worked at the sewing room, 12-year old daughter Rosa Mae was tasked with looking after her siblings when not at school. A neighbor kept the baby until Rosa Mae came home. When asked what she wanted Santa Claus to bring her for Christmas, she replied "James and Edwin need pants lots worse than I need things."[28]

By 1940, sewing room workers had made 2,341,369 garments and 130,408 household articles.[29] By this time, the number of women enrolled in the program had dropped to 650 ranging in age from 35 to 64 years.[30] That same year, the sewing rooms were at the center of attention when WPA administrators in Washington ruled that local communities had to bear more of the cost of operating the program by providing the material used in the sewing rooms. Up to that point, the City of Fort Worth had provided some supplies such as thread.[31] Communities in Texas balked at this added expense, claiming that the cost would place additional strains on already stretched local governments. In Fort Worth, conformity with the ruling would require at least an additional $40,000 a year. Local officials admitted that compliance would cost less than supporting the workers who would be placed on direct relief roles. Eventually, city and county authorities chose to comply with the federal order.[32]

Although WPA administrators looked at employment at a sewing room as a means of providing a woman with the type of homemaking training that would allow her to meet her family's needs, the skills learned in the sewing rooms proved to be transferable. Fort Worth had numerous garment-making factories at the time, including the Williamson-Dickie Company and the Dickson-Jenkins Company, both manufacturers of work clothing. From 1936 until 1941, Amy Opal Burns worked in a Fort Worth sewing room. She was the economic head of a household with five children and a disabled husband. In addition to working there, her family was also the recipient of goods made in the sewing room. As American involvement in World War II became more evident, she then found employment at Williamson-Dickie as the company focused its efforts on making uniforms for the military. She stayed with the firm as it transitioned from war- to peace-time production. She retired from Williamson-Dickie in 1966.[33]

WPA sewing rooms in Fort Worth remained in operation until the summer of 1942 when they were disbanded.[34] As the United States geared up for World War II, many women, such as Amy Opal Burns, were able to find better paying jobs in defense-related industries. As an agency, the WPA was abolished in 1943 as the country emerged from the Depression into a war-time economy with virtually full employment. For the seven years that Fort Worth's sewing rooms functioned, the women who worked in them produced an abundance of essential goods for needy individuals, provided some economic relief for themselves and their families, and gained a sense of self-worth and comradery among their co-workers. Yet there is little left to remind us of their important work with the exception of a few repurposed buildings.[35]

10.4   Opal Herd is shown making a pattern for a size 34 dress. Courtesy "Texas and the WPA" (www.flickr.com).

Notes and Acknowledgments

[1] For more information on WPA and other New Deal-related sites in Texas and other states, check the projects lists available on the website of the Living New Deal, www.livingnewdeal.org/projects. Projects can be searched by state and city, project type (i.e., Archeology and History, Art, Civic Facilities, Education and Health, etc.), and by New Deal agency. As of September 16, 2018, 806 projects in Texas, both extant and demolished, have been documented in the organization's online database.

[2] *Handbook of Texas Online*, Mallory B. Randle, "Work Projects Administration," (http://www.tshaonline.org/handbook/online/rticles/new01), accessed September 10, 2018; Federal Works Agency, Work Projects Administration, Report on Progress of the WPA Program, June 30, 1940, pp. 39 and 62.

[3] Security, Work, and Relief Policies: Report of the Committee on Long-Range Work and Relief Policies to the National Resources Planning Board (Washington, DC: Government Printing Office, 1942), p. 43, footnote 10, p. 44, footnote 20, p. 64, footnote 6, and p. 128, (http://infoweb.newsbank.com/gbnl/documents), accessed January 24, 2013.

[4] "The State Press: The Sewing Rooms," *Dallas Morning News*, July 31, 1936, p. 18; "Sewing Room Checks to be Issued Later," *Dallas Morning News*, December 19, 1936, p.4; "Sewing Room Needs Work," *Dallas Morning News*, October 19, 1937, p. 12; "Sewing Quarters at Throckmorton Moved," *Fort Worth Star-Telegram*, May 11, 1938, p. 2; "$812,875 for WPA Approved," *Fort Worth Star-Telegram*, August 27, 1935, p. 4.

[5] Mary Wynn, "Plenty of Oomph Boasted by Sewing Room Garments," *Fort Worth Star-Telegram* (morning edition), May 7, 1939, AR406 7-195-100, *Fort Worth Star-Telegram* Clippings Collection, Special Collections, University of Texas at Arlington Library [hereafter cited as FWSTCC/SCUTA].

[6] "WPA Sewing Room and Home Economic Project to Hold Open House Tomorrow," *Fort Worth Star-Telegram* (morning edition), March 9, 1937, AR406-7-195-100, FWSTCC/SCUTA; Wynn, "Plenty of Oomph Boasted by Sewing Room Garments."

[7] Wynn, "Plenty of Oomph Boasted by Sewing Room Garments."

[8] "WPA Sewing Room and Home Economic Project to Hold Open House Tomorrow."

[9] "WPA Sewing Room Turns Out Expert Housekeepers," *Fort Worth Star-Telegram*, March 28, 1937, p. 2; Amy Boyd Chamberlin, "Why Should Groundhogs Control Our Weather? Are We Mice or Men? Arise!—Arise!—Arise!," *Fort Worth Star-Telegram*, February 6, 1938, p. 40; Wynn, "Plenty of Oomph Boasted by Sewing Room Garments."

[10] "WPA Sewing Room Turns Out Expert Housekeepers." The African American porter is shown in Picture No. S-6837, January 14, 1941, Texas Work Projects Administration, Record Group 69, Records of the Work Projects Administration, National Archives and Records Administration, College Park, Maryland, (https://www.flickr.com/photos/141324854@N04/albums

/72157666432899962, accessed September 17, 2018.)

¹¹ Julia Kirk Blackwelder, *Women of the Depression: Caste and Culture in San Antonio, 1929-1939* (College Station: Texas A&M University Press, 1984), p. 123.

¹² On several occasions, the *Fort Worth Star-Telegram* specifically mentioned that there were separate sewing rooms for whites and blacks. Only one reference to Mexican American sewing room workers has been found in the Fort Worth Star-Telegram and the inference from that article is that they worked alongside whites. See "WPA Sewing Room and Home Economic Project to Hold Open House Tomorrow."

¹³ "Building is Renovated for WPA Sewing Room," *Fort Worth Star-Telegram*, November 7, 1936, p. 18.

¹⁴ P. J. Conway to D. L. Lewis, February 14, 1939, Series I: Mayor and Council Proceedings, 1939, Box 1, Council Proceedings, February 1939, Fort Worth Library Archives, Fort Worth, Texas.

¹⁵ List of city council directives from October 12, 1938 to March 22, 1939, Series I: Mayor and Council Proceedings, 1939, Box 1, Council Proceedings, March 1939, Fort Worth Library Archives, Fort Worth, Texas. A directive for February 15, 1939 was recorded as "City Manager to submit cost of constructing building on city owned land to house W.P.A. sewing room workers."

¹⁶ "New Sewing Room Location Chosen," *Fort Worth Star-Telegram* (morning edition), February 25, 1939, AR406-7-195-102, FWSTCC/SCUTA.

¹⁷ Wynn, "Plenty of Oomph Boasted by Sewing Room Garments." In conjunction with written descriptions, historic photographs provide excellent documentation as to how the sewing rooms operated. One of the best sources is found in Record Group 69, Records of the Work Projects Administration, National Archives and Records Administration, College Park, Maryland. Fortunately for Texans interested in the WPA, staff from the Historic Sites and Structures Program, Texas Parks and Wildlife Department, scanned thousands of images, including labels on the backs of the photos, pertaining to WPA and PWA (Public Works Administration) projects in the state. These images are now available on the internet through the photo-sharing website, Flickr (www.flickr.com) under the title Texas and the WPA. Photographs are grouped in albums by county names. Many of these albums contain images of sewing rooms that operated in the state. Photographs of Fort Worth's sewing rooms are available at https://www.flickr.com/photos/141324854@N04/albums/72157666432899962.

¹⁸ Wynn, "Plenty of Oomph Boasted by Sewing Room Garments."

¹⁹ "'What'll We Do,' Ask Sewers, 'If Room is Closed,'" *Fort Worth Star-Telegram* (morning edition), July 11, 1940, AR406-7-195-103, FWSTCC/SCUTA.

²⁰ Felix R. McKnight, "Camp Wolters Soldiers Won't Lack Recreation; Citizens of Mineral Wells to Open Center," *Dallas Morning News*, June 13, 1941, p. 9.

²¹ Wynn, "Plenty of Oomph Boasted by Sewing Room Garments."

²² "WPA Means, 'We Patch Anything' at Sewing Rooms," *Fort Worth Star-Telegram* (evening edition), February 21, 1936, AR606 7-195-100, FWSTCC/ SCUTA.

²³ "WPA Sewing Room Turns Out Expert Housekeepers."

²⁴ Chamberlin, "Why Should Groundhogs Control Our Weather?"

[25] "WPA Sewing Room and Home Economics Project to Hold Open House Tomorrow."; "WPA Ready for Open House," *Fort Worth Star-Telegram*, May 20, 1940, p. 14.

[26] "WPA Sewing Room Worker is Robbed of Her Last Dime," *Fort Worth Star-Telegram*, August 15, 1936, p. 1.

[27] "Boy, 7, Wants Clothes Worse Than Toys," *Fort Worth Star-Telegram*, December 18, 1936, p. 10; Jerry Flemmons, Amon: *The Life of Amon Carter of Texas* (Austin, Texas: Jenkins Publishing Company, 1978), p. 391.

[28] Katherine Alexander, "Basement is Haven for Five," *Fort Worth Star-Telegram*, December 16, 1937, p. 16.

[29] "Report of WPA Work is Made," *Fort Worth Star-Telegram* (evening edition), March 24, 1940, AR406-7-195-103, FWSTCC/ SCUTA.

[30] "'What'll We Do,' Ask Sewers, 'If Room is Closed.'"

[31] G. L. Cline to D. L. Lewis, October 5, 1938, Series I: Mayor and Council Proceedings, 1938, Box 2, Council Proceedings, October 1938, Fort Worth Library Archives, Fort Worth, Texas. Six local department stores were given the opportunity to offer a quote on thread but declined to do so.

[32] "WPA Sewing Room May Be Closed," *Fort Worth Star-Telegram* (morning edition), July 10, 1940, "Sewing Rooms May Continue as at Present," *Fort Worth Star-Telegram* (evening edition), July 12, 1940, and "Sewing Room Goods Ordered," *Fort Worth Star-Telegram* (evening edition), July 30, 1940, AR406-7-195-103, FWSTCC/ SCUTA. For an account of the reaction of communities in Texas' WPA District 7 (which included Fort Worth and numerous counties to the west) to the federal order, see, E. D. Alexander, "Congress to Get Sewing Room Plea," *Fort Worth Star-Telegram*, July 16, 1940, section 2, p. 1.

[33] Interview with James R. Burns, Jr., April 28, 2005 (notes in the possession of the author); Entry for Amy O. Burns, 1940 U. S. Census. (https://search.ancestry.com/cgi-bin/sse.dll?indiv=1&db=1940usfedcen&h=160356084), accessed September 9, 2018; Bill Fairley, "Everyone helped during the Depression," *Fort Worth Star-Telegram*, August 27, 2005, 6B.

[34] "Fort Worth Now Port of Entry by Air," *Fort Worth Star-Telegram*, August 6, 1942, p. 9.

[35] Unfortunately, the Kingsbury Building, the location of the African American sewing room, was demolished. The building at 610 W. Daggett Street still functions as the headquarters for Justin Boots and was listed in the National Register of Historic Places in 2017 as a contributing resource in the Jennings-Vickery Historic District. The Parker-Browne Company Building was individually listed in the National Register in 2015, in part, because of its significance as the location of a WPA sewing room. The current author wrote that nomination and it provided the impetus and some of the content for this article. She wishes to thank Seth J. Adams and Fran McCarthy for bringing the project her way.

Texas Historical Memory: The Curious Case of the Princeton FSA Migratory Labor Camp

Keith Volanto

Located forty miles to the northeast of Dallas along U.S. Highway 380, the town of Princeton is a growing community seeking to diversify from a solely agricultural past. As local leaders seek to attract newcomers to bolster the tax base, older residents continue to take pride in their town's history. One way in which they have done so is by actively promoting their community park as the site of a former World War II prisoner-of-war camp. Through a multitude of conspicuous road signs marked with the label "WW II P.O.W. camp" directing potential visitors to the site, a large entrance sign with the prison camp prominently displayed in the park's official title, and references to the P.O.W. camp on the town government's web pages, it is not hard for a casual witness to perceive how the community seeks to claim the location as a place of historical significance due to its contribution to the war effort. A closer examination of the site's true history, however, produces a fuller, much richer story.[1]

Only a few camp remnants are still visible today, most notably its tall, rusty water tower overlooking the main public area which hosts a collection of softball fields, a concession stand, covered eating pavilion, and a nearby parking lot. Some distance away, old concrete slabs which originally served as foundations for tents and cabins also remain, largely repurposed to support barbeque grills for picnic goers. A Texas Historical Commission marker attached to the dining pavilion attempts to explain the importance of the park site as a WW II P.O.W. Camp, but in the process, reveals something even more significant, that a Depression-era migrant labor camp existed there first, and later, for over twenty years after the war concluded:

SITE OF WORLD WAR II PRISONER OF WAR CAMP

Here in 1941, with the Hon. Sam Rayburn, Speaker of the U.S. House of Representatives, in attendance, a migratory labor camp was dedicated. With the coming of World War II later in the decade, however, federal officials converted the site for use as a camp to hold German prisoners of war. While here, the German soldiers worked on Princeton area farms, providing valuable labor assistance. For many years following the prisoners' release in 1946, the site again served as a camp for migrant workers.[2]

Not only does the marker inflate the site's significance—neglecting to explain that rather than being an extensive facility such as Camp Hearne which held thousands of German prisoners throughout the war, Princeton served as a small, agricultural branch camp that funneled about a hundred German P.O.W.s to nearby farms for only a single growing season in 1945—the marker's text also completely diminishes the location's extensive use before, during, and after the war as a migrant labor camp, treating that part of the story as a mere footnote when one could argue, as I will in this essay, that it is actually the site's primary historical importance.

Migrant labor camps arose in Texas and other states across the country during the Great Depression as a result of two complementary impulses: the presence of a large, mobile rural labor force in search of both work and sanitary living spaces, coupled with the need of agricultural producers for a steady supply of workers to maintain and harvest their crops, a demand made even more imperative as a result of wartime labor shortages. Initiated by the Resettlement Administration, later known as the Farm Security Administration (FSA), the Migratory Labor Camp Program, which operated from 1935 to 1946, began in California as a response to the crush of poor white Dust Bowl migrants pouring into the state by the mid-1930s, in an effort to provide safe and clean facilities for laborers and a stable system of recruitment and distribution of farm workers for agricultural landowners. Made famous by John Steinbeck's *The Grapes of Wrath* and its subsequent Hollywood portrayal, the migrant labor program expanded to 95 camps by the early 1940s, with nine located in Texas. The Princeton camp became the northeastern-most location along the "Big Swing"—the cotton-picking circuit that many migrant workers followed northward as the crops harvested beginning with the fields of the Lower Rio Grande Valley of south Texas.[3]

Prior to the establishment of the formal camps, large numbers of migrant workers during the Depression congregated in makeshift encampments of their own creation, living out of their jalopies or tents set up along county roads or more secluded areas off the beaten path, often with abysmal sanitary conditions and no educational opportunities for the workers' children. Public efforts during the early 1930s to end these "squatters' camps" by creating living space for migrants in county fairgrounds or empty town lots proved to be completely inadequate. FSA officials began to assert the need for formal camps, not only as a more efficient way to alleviate glaring health-related issues while matching landowners with potential employees, but also as an important means of tempering crime and potential labor unrest if the increasingly unacceptable situation continued.[4]

The first FSA camp constructed in Texas, located in Raymondville, was completed in 1939, along with three other south Texas camps. By the end of 1941, five additional camps were built in the Lone Star State, including the camp in Princeton, which was secured after a visit by FSA officials and meetings with local leaders in the fall of 1939.[5]

Positioned along the migratory trail, the Princeton FSA camp handled the flow of farm workers and distributed them to meet the needs of local employers. The camp required all those residing to formally register on site with the United States Employment Service office responsible for labor placement on the cotton and onion farms in the Princeton area. While this arrangement provided workers and employers with a more stable system of labor management, allowing government agents to intercede in this manner did result in the migrants relinquishing some of their negotiating power for better working conditions.[6]

The FSA migrant camps existed as far more than mere labor concentration and distribution centers. Indeed, Farm Security Administration officials actively sought to provide protected shelters and valuable social services while attempting to foster a strong sense of community for the workers. While a marked improvement over the improvised worker-created shelters of the pre-camp era, housing at the Princeton camp was quite modest, consisting of concrete bases with simple wood cabins or tents placed upon them. Nevertheless, migrants would find nearby privies, communal showers, laundry facilities, and fresh water drinking fountains. Unlike the other FSA camps in Texas which primarily housed Hispanic workers, the Princeton camp frequently contained significant numbers of Anglo migrants, leading FSA officials to informally segregate residents into separate living areas for each racial group.[7]

Obsessed with containing the spread of disease, the FSA maintained a health clinic at all of their camps. A nurse who lived on-site ran the clinic at Princeton, aided by local doctors who contracted with the FSA to visit the camp regularly to treat sick or injured workers and provide valuable preventative care. The nurse and a committee of residents would also hold frequent health inspections of living quarters and deal with any specific issues of concern. In one instance, after encountering trouble maintaining the privies and showers, a special committee was formed to institute a cleanup campaign whereby the cleanest camp districts were awarded white flags to proudly display while the dirtiest district would be publicly shamed by being forced to unfurl a black flag until the next inspection the following week.[8]

Community-building efforts by the FSA fostered numerous social uplift opportunities for the residents. The Princeton camp's community hall (where the current covered dining pavilion and historical marker are located) provided the focal point of social interaction. Frequent dances, concerts, and movie screenings held at the hall offered the primary attraction for large numbers of camp residents to congregate. Any important meeting called by the camp director that required everyone's attention took place at the hall. The location also served as the meeting place for the resident Camp Council and the assortment of camp committees formed to foster positive relationships as well as deal with a variety of community issues. The council and committees worked with FSA administrators to enforce camp rules and institute discipline, police the site, organize entertainment events, maintain sanitary conditions, and to run the *Princeton Farm Workers Weekly*, the camp's newspaper. Encouraging participation in camp administration was seen by FSA leaders as an important means of directly investing residents in the well-being of their community, while reaffirming American democracy. As Princeton camp manager James H. Martin wrote:

> All of us have to know our Council better. It is foremostly one of the most important things about a community. It is our little side-bet against dictatorships and Hitlers. Next to giving housing to the depressed folks in agriculture we believe in giving democracy and health as the next important items. Health and housing don't mean much without democracy. It is through our Council that we will get the most constructive work done for whatever we will try to do in the months to come. They are our government, and the manager will back them up in what they decide with the people's consent and will.[9]

For four years during World War II, the camp housed the migrant workers who contributed greatly to the local economy as they toiled for long hours in the hot Princeton-area fields, planting and harvesting cotton and onion crops before returning to the camp to rest from a long day's work, tend to their families' needs, and commiserate with other members of the community. As wartime demands gradually led to a great reduction of available laborers, federal government officials made the decision to convert the Princeton facility into a prisoner of war camp for captured German soldiers. The site was used as a temporary camp for the 1945 season, housing the prisoners who were funneled to the fields previously worked by the migrants. After the war, the Germans returned home and, for the next twenty years, the site once again served as a migrant labor camp, though supervised by state authorities after the Farm Security Administration was disbanded in 1946.[10]

When mechanized agriculture and other changes led to the end of migrant labor in North Texas by the mid-1960s, the abandoned camp site fell victim to the elements and became a dilapidated eyesore. The Princeton Housing Authority and city officials under the leadership of Mayor J.M. Caldwell cleaned up the site in 1969, tearing down the remaining buildings and cabins, hauling away whatever was not buried or burned. The move was celebrated in the local press at the time as part of a Princeton's efforts to "step forward" as it began to move away from its previous dependence upon agriculture. he old camp site was envisioned as the future site of either a public park or a community college, while a recently completed "ultra-modern" water and sewage project, a new high school, and additional land annexations, it was hoped, would attract fresh tax-paying homeowners to Princeton, touted as a "most desirable place to live and to rear a family." In 1986, the site finally became the community park it is today— the "J.M. Caldwell, Sr. Community Park/ WW II P.O.W. Camp"—with its historical marker dedicated at a highly publicized Fourth of July gala featuring a patriotic program and fireworks.[11]

The town's collective memory with respect to the old site as primarily being a World War II POW camp needs to be viewed within this lens of local boosterism. While never completely ignoring mention of the migrant labor camp, the efforts to gin up patriotic pride while diminishing its agriculture past, as mentioned in the introduction, are ubiquitous. Many articles appearing in area newspapers over the years, as well as a recent video produced by the nearby City of Plano, relay stories of the German prisoners coming to town and helping the wartime economy of

North Texas with only casual mention of the place as a migrant camp other than that it existed on the site beforehand. Seemingly, the site's previous use as a migrant labor camp during World War II, and for over two decades afterwards, had no historical importance other than being the reason why the P.O.W. camp was located there.[12]

The fact that professional historians have not yet researched the Princeton camp in order to produce a more accurate counter-narrative is another element contributing to this collective historical amnesia. Early local enthusiasts who framed the initial story of the site and its presumed value were amateur historians who dismissed the migrant camp's existence as not historically significant. Those interested in promoting local history in subsequent years have likewise been similarly untrained in formal historical study. A prime example of this comes from a 2003 local article in which a self-proclaimed researcher and publisher of Collin County history is quoted as saying that she has tried to track down records of the Princeton P.O.W. camp as well as the men who stayed there, but it could not be done because "locally, no one kept track of the paperwork," which is an outrageous statement to the eyes and ears of any professional scholar with knowledge of the period. The National Archives in College Park, Maryland, in fact, holds the U.S. military's records from World War II and certainly would have the rosters of prisoners and countless other valuable documents that would tell the story of that part of the camp's existence. More important, however, is that Record Group 96 at the same facility also houses the files of the Princeton migrant labor camp, at least during the Farm Security Administration years. When properly researched, these records will provide extensive evidence to relate the experiences of the migrant workers who lived at the site from 1941 to 1945. Ultimately, how a community chooses to remember historical sites and noteworthy figures often has a greater impact on the collective memory of the local populace than any work of history produced by a professional historian, but on topics receiving no scholarly treatment, the hold of historical memory is even more susceptible to those more interested in promoting a self-interested narrative over one that is more historically accurate.[13]

Though the general story of the Princeton site as both a former migrant camp and a P.O.W. camp has been relayed to the public, the order of significance, such as displayed on the existing historical marker, is clearly skewed and needs to be recalibrated. Rather than appearing as a footnote, the site's use as a lively and much longer-lasting migrant labor camp should receive primary emphasis, far outweighing the ancillary side story of the place's relatively brief use as an agricultural branch camp for German P.O.W.s at the tail end of World War II. A more balanced historical representation would mention the P.O.W. camp experience, but also prioritize the experiences of the migrants who lived there and worked nearby for a much longer period of time, appearing something such as the following:

SITE OF FSA MIGRANT LABOR CAMP

Here in 1941, with the Hon. Sam Rayburn, Speaker of the US House of Representatives in attendance, a migratory labor camp was dedicated. During the Great Depression and World War II, a vibrant community of workers lived here in safe and sanitary conditions provided by the Farm Security Administration, which also helped them find work picking cotton and onions for Princeton-area farm owners.

Near the end of WW II, German POWs briefly housed here performed similar work. After the war, the camp was used again by migrant workers, who continued to contribute to the local economy for the next 25 years.

The case of the Princeton migrant labor camp is not entirely unique in Texas historical memory. The Crystal City camp in south Texas has received similar treatment, in that, on its historical marker the site's origin as a migrant camp is also briefly mentioned before being largely supplanted by extensive space devoted to its later use as a major wartime Immigration and Naturalization Service enemy alien detention facility. It should be noted, however, that unlike the Princeton camp, the Crystal City facility operated much longer than eight months, with many Japanese and Germans and some Italians being held there for six years. The location also did not revert back to its prewar use as a migrant camp after the war. Nevertheless, two other former migrant camp sites that were not converted to other purposes during the war— Robstown in South Texas, and Lamesa in northwest Texas—both have Texas Historical Commission markers dedicated to their FSA and post-FSA days, reaffirming the ideal that long-lasting migrant labor camps have historical significance in their own right, even if a German prisoner never set foot on its grounds.[14]

Notes and Acknowledgments

[1] The population of Princeton has grown rapidly in the 21st century, from 3,477 in 2000 to over 10,000 by 2018. In 1930, Princeton had only 459 residents.

[2] Texas Historical Commission Marker, Atlas Number 5085006222. For the text and specific information about other historical markers in Texas, visit the THC's Marker Atlas at https://atlas.thc.state.tx.us.

[3] Verónica Martínez-Matsuda, "Making the Modern Migrant: Work, Community, and Struggle in the Federal Migrant Labor Camp Program, 1935-1947," Ph.D. diss. (University of Texas, 2009): 5-8. For the history of the Resettlement Administration/Farm Security Administration, see: Sidney Baldwin, *Poverty and Politics: The Rise and Decline of the Farm Security Administration* (Chapel Hill: University of North Carolina Press, 1968); Paul E. Mertz, *New Deal Policy and Southern Rural Poverty* (Baton Rouge: Louisiana State University Press, 1978); Theodore Saloutos, *The New Deal and the American Farmer* (Ames: Iowa State University Press, 1982).

[4] W.A. Canon (FSA Assistant Regional Director) to Arthur C. Petermann (FSA Oklahoma State Director), February 5, 1942, in January 1942 folder, Box 1, Records of the Office of the Region 8 Director, General Correspondence, 1935-1942, Farmers Home Administration Records, National Archives at Fort Worth, Texas (hereafter FHA Records, NA-Fort Worth); Martínez-Matsuda, "Making the Modern Migrant," 36-43.

[5] B.J. Walker (FSA Labor Representative) to Mercer G. Evans (FSA Personnel and Labor Relations Division Director), September 8, 1939, in July 1938-September 1939 folder, Box 1, FHA Records, NA-Fort Worth; Martínez-Matsuda, "Making the Modern Migrant," 49-58.

[6] Martínez-Matsuda, "Making the Modern Migrant," 58-59; Emilio Zamora, *The World of the Mexican Worker in Texas* (College Station: Texas A&M University Press), 30.

[7] Martínez-Matsuda, "Making the Modern Migrant," 146-48.

[8] Martínez-Matsuda, "Making the Modern Migrant," 224. For details on the Farm Security Administration's health programs, see: Brenda Jeanette Taylor, "The Farm Security Administration: Meeting Rural Health Needs in the South, 1933-1946," (Ph.D. diss., Texas Christian University); Michael R. Grey, *New Deal Medicine: The Rural Health Programs of the Farm Security Administration* (Baltimore: Johns Hopkins University Press, 1999); T.R. Clark, "The Limits of State Autonomy: The Medical Cooperatives of the Farm Security Administration, 1935-1946," *Journal of Policy History*, vol. 11, no. 3 (1999), 257-82.

[9] James H. Martin quoted in Martínez-Matsuda, "Making the Modern Migrant," 257-58, from the January 28, 1942 issue of the Princeton Farm Workers Weekly, Record Group 96 files, National Archives, College Park, Maryland.

[10] Historical Marker Application for "Site of World War II Prisoner of War Camp, Princeton, Collin County," Texas Historical Commission. For

information on German POWs in Texas, see: Arnold P. Krammer, "When the Afrika Korps Came to Texas," *Southwestern Historical Quarterly* 80 (January 1977); Robert Tissing, "Stalag Texas, 1943–1945," *Military History of Texas and the Southwest* 13 (Fall 1976); and Richard Paul Walker, Prisoners of War in Texas during World War II (Ph.D. dissertation, North Texas State University, 1980).

[11] "Princeton Spruces Up," *McKinney Courier-Gazette*, November 7, 1969; "City Needs to Spruce Up before July 4th Bash," Princeton Herald, June 26, 1987; "6,000 Enjoy July 4 Bash at Community Park," Princeton Herald, July 9, 1987.

[12] "Luftwaffe Pilot Returns to Princeton POW campsite," *Princeton Herald*, April 11, 1983; "Princeton's WWII German POW Camp Transformed into a Community Park," Wylie News, November 8, 2006; "Princeton, Texas POW Camp," accessed August 23, 2018 at https://www.youtube.com/watch?v=GrGMbQvpON8.

[13] "Local WW II POW Camps Disappear without a Trace," *North Texas e-News* (Bonham), July 27, 2003.

[14] For a brief introduction to the Crystal City camp and the variety of civilian prisoners held there, see *Handbook of Texas Online*, Emily Brosveen, "WORLD WAR II INTERNMENT CAMPS," accessed Sept. 7, 2018, http://www.tshaonline.org/handbook/online/articles/quwby.

Notes on Contributors

Cynthia Brandimarte earned a PhD in American Studies at the University of Texas at Austin. She worked with regional historical societies and museums throughout Texas before joining Texas State Parks (TPWD) as Director of the Historic Sites and Structures Program (retired 2018). She has authored two award winning books, *Inside Texas: Culture, Identity and Houses, 1878-1920* and *Texas State Parks and the CCC: the Legacy of the Civilian Conservation Corps*

Carroll Scogin-Brincefield grew up in Corpus Christi, Texas, and received her B.S. and M.A. degrees in history from Central Missouri State University. She retired as Chief Appraiser/Tax Collector for Concho County and now resides in Lavaca County, where she is working as an independent historian and researcher. Carroll is President of the South Texas Historical Association. She dedicates her study of the National Youth Administration to her father, Lem R. Scoggin and her aunt, Ruth Luder Stevens.

Carolyn A. Carroll received her M.A. in History from Sam Houston State University where she is a Lecturer in the History Department. She is Adjunct Faculty of History at Lone Star College, Conroe, and an active member of the Montgomery County Historical Society.

George M. Cooper is Adjunct Professor of History, Lone Star College, Montgomery, and teaches History at Blinn College, Bryan. He is Past President of the East Texas Historical Association and the South Texas Historical Association, holding the positions simultaneously. George is a Fellow of the East Texas Historical Association and Convener of the Texas New Deal Symposium. An earlier version of his paper appeared in The Journal of South Texas, Fall, 2015, and is used with permission.

Light T. Cummins is Bryan Professor of History at Austin College, Sherman, Texas, and a member of the Texas Institute of Letters and the Philosophical Society of Texas. Cummins, a Fellow of the East Texas Historical Association, served as the official State Historian of Texas from 2009 to 2011. He is the author of the award-winning *Emily Austin of Texas*, 1795-1851 and the biography of New Deal-era artist Allie Victoria Tennant.

Victoria H. Cummins, Dr. A.M. Pate Professor of History at Austin College, teaches courses in Latin American history and the history of women. She holds a Ph.D. from Tulane University. Her current research deals with the role of women in Texas regional art. She has published articles based on this research including "Women Artists and the Public Works of Art Project" and "Art in Your Backyard: The Public Works of Art Project in Small Towns in East Texas."

Ronald E. Goodwin is Associate Professor at Prairie View A&M University. He completed his undergraduate degree at Texas Lutheran University while serving on active duty in the U.S. Air Force. After his honorable discharge, Ron completed graduate degrees at Texas Southern University. He is the author of *Remembering the Days of Sorry: The WPA and the Texas Slave Narratives*.

Milton S. Jordan is a retired United Methodist Pastor and an avocational historian. He has a B.A. in History from Southwestern University and a Master of Divinity from SMU. Jordan is a Past President and a Fellow of the East Texas Historical Association. He has edited several works on Texas History, including *Just Between Us: Stories and Memories from the Texas Pines*, with Dan K. Utley.

Susan Allen Kline, an independent historian in Fort Worth, specializes in the documentation of the built environment. Her work has appeared in *The Chronicles of Oklahoma* and *Legacies: A History Journal for Dallas and North Central Texas*. Susan is the recipient of the Texas State Historical Association's Cecilia Steinfeldt Fellowship and the co-author of *Fort Worth Parks*.

Jeffrey L. Littlejohn serves as Professor of History at Sam Houston State University in Huntsville, Texas. His latest essay, "The Cabiness Family Lynching: Race War and Memory in Walker County, Texas" appeared in the *Southwestern Historical Quarterly*, July 2018. It received the Texas State Historical Association's Special Award for Research and Writing on Texas in World War I. Littlejohn's other publications and digital projects may be accessed at http//www.studythepast.org.

Brenda Taylor Matthews is A.M. Pate Chair of History at Texas Wesleyan University, where she has taught for 23 years. Her B.S. is from Dallas Baptist University and she earned both her M.A. and Ph.D. from Texas Christian University. She held a Fulbright professorship at the University of Stuttgart, 1998-1999. In addition to her research in rural New Deal programs, she has written articles on the WPA state guides.

Mary L. Scheer is Professor of History and Director of the Center for Culture and History at Lamar University in Beaumont, Texas. She received a B.A. and M.A. from Texas State University and a Ph.D. from Texas Christian University. She is a former Fulbright Scholar in Germany and author/editor of five academic books on Texas and women's history. Dr. Scheer is Past President and a Fellow of the East Texas Historical Association.

Keith Volanto received his Ph.D. in History from Texas A&M University. He is the author of *Texas, Cotton, and the New Deal*, as well as ten scholarly articles on the New Deal experience in Texas. He is currently Professor of History at Collin College in Plano, Texas.

Kyle Wilkison received his Ph.D. in History from Vanderbilt University. He is the author of the award-winning book *Yeomen, Sharecroppers, and Socialists: Plain Folk Protest in Texas*, 1870-1914, and is a Past President and Fellow of the East Texas Historical Association.

www.ingramcontent.com/pod-product-compliance
Lightning Source LLC
Chambersburg PA
CBHW060528080526
44586CB00012B/657